Japanese Public Sentiment on South Korea

The contributors to this book demonstrate empirically how Japanese public opinion is formed amid strained Japan–South Korea relations.

Studying public opinion in Japan and South Korea is critically important for exploring the causes and consequences of the deterioration of the relationship between the two countries. Japan–South Korea relations are at their worst level since World War II. Faced with North Korea's nuclear threat and China's regional and global advances, Japan and South Korea are each allied with the US and function as key stabilizers within the Asia–Pacific "Pax Americana." These relations play a decisive role in East Asia's international security.

The contributors explore a variety of social scientific methodologies—both conventional quantitative surveys and online survey experiments, as well as quantitative text analyses of published books and computational analyses of social media data—to disentangle the dynamic relationship between Japanese public opinion and Japan–South Korea relations.

An invaluable resource for scholars of East Asian regional security issues.

Tetsuro Kobayashi is Associate Professor in the Department of Media and Communication at City University of Hong Kong.

Atsushi Tago is Professor in the School of Political Science and Economics at Waseda University, Tokyo, Japan and Global Fellow of Peace Research Institute Oslo (PRIO), Norway.

Politics in Asia series

Deliberative Democracy in Asia
Baogang He, Michael Breen and James Fishkin

Chinese Foreign Policy Toward the Middle East
Kadir Temiz

Decolonizing Central Asian International Relation
Beyond Empires
Timur Dadabaev

Russia in the Indo-Pacific
New Approaches to Russian Foreign Policy
Gaye Christoffersen

China and Human Rights in North Korea
Debating a "Developmental Approach" in Northeast Asia

The Volatility and Future of Democracies in Asia
Hsin-Huang Michael Hsiao and Alan Hao Yang

Chinese Election Interference in Taiwan
Edward Barss

Japanese Public Sentiment on South Korea
Popular Opinion and International Relations
Edited by Tetsuro Kobayashi and Atsushi Tago

For more information about this series, please visit:
https://www.routledge.com/Politics-in-Asia/book-series/PIA

Japanese Public Sentiment on South Korea

Popular Opinion and
International Relations

**Edited by Tetsuro Kobayashi
and Atsushi Tago**

LONDON AND NEW YORK

First published 2022
by Routledge
2 Park Square, Milton Park, Abingdon, Oxon OX14 4RN

and by Routledge
605 Third Avenue, New York, NY 10158

Routledge is an imprint of the Taylor & Francis Group, an informa business

British Library Cataloguing-in-Publication Data
A catalogue record for this book is available from the British Library

Library of Congress Cataloging-in-Publication Data
A catalog record has been requested for this book

ISBN: 978-0-367-69849-2 (hbk)
ISBN: 978-0-367-69848-5 (pbk)
ISBN: 978-1-003-14353-6 (ebk)

DOI: 10.4324/9781003143536

Typeset in Galliard
by KnowledgeWorks Global Ltd.

Contents

Contributors' Biographies

Yuki Asaba is a Professor at Doshisha University Faculty of Global and Regional Studies, Kyoto, Japan. He is also an adjunct professor at the University of North Korean Studies, Seoul, Korea. While he teaches the Korean language in the classroom, he keenly recognizes the generation/gender gap in Japanese perceptions of Korea.

Shohei Doi is an Associate Professor of International Relations at the School of Law and the Public Policy School, Hokkaido University. He obtained a Ph.D. in Political Science in 2019 from Kyoto University. He has published in *PLOS ONE* and the *Journal of Computational Social Science*. His research interests cover the intersection between international politics/security and economy.

Kyu S. Hahn is a Professor of Communication at Seoul National University. His research examines the effects of media in the political process, primarily with massive behavioral data. His works have appeared in *Journal of Communication*, *Public Opinion Quarterly*, *Political Communication*, *British Journal of Political Science*, and *Journal of Politics*. He has also published in *Computational Statistics* and *Journal of Applied Statistics*. He has published over 400 data journalism articles collaborating with major news outlets in South Korea. Currently, as a Guest Editorial Writer, he contributes a monthly column to the Donga Ilbo.

Kaori Hayashi is a Professor of Media and Journalism Studies at the Graduate School of Interdisciplinary Information Studies, the University of Tokyo. Her most recent English publications include "The Silent Public in a Liberal State: Challenges for Japan's Journalism in the Age of the Internet" in *The Crisis of Liberal Internationalism. Japan and the World Order*. Edited by Yoichi Funabashi and G. John Ikenberry. Brookings Institution Press, 2020, 325–358. For her publication list and recent activities, please see: http://www.hayashik.iii.u-tokyo.ac.jp.

Kazunori Inamasu is a Professor of Social Psychology at the School of Sociology, Kwansei Gakuin University. He received a Ph.D. in Social Psychology from the University of Tokyo in 2013. His research focuses on the relationship between media and public opinion. He has published articles in journals such as *Political Communication*, the *Japanese Journal of Social Psychology*, and *Japanese Electoral Studies*.

Tetsuro Kobayashi is an Associate Professor at the Department of Media and Communication, City University of Hong Kong. His research revolves around political communication, political psychology, and public opinion in East Asia. His recent work has been published in journals such as *Communication Research*, *New Media & Society*, and the *Journal of Cross-Cultural Psychology*.

Shoko Kohama is an Associate Professor of International Relations at the Public Policy School, Hokkaido University. Her Ph.D. in Foreign Affairs was conferred by the University of Virginia. She has published works in journals such as *Political Communication*, and *International Relations of the Asia-Pacific*. Her research primarily explores ways to restore peace and prosperity in the aftermath of interstate and civil wars.

Hongchun Lee is a Professor at the Department of College of Humanities at Dongguk University, South Korea. He specializes in International communication and Internet election campaigns in South Korea. His recent works include Kim, T. & Lee, H. (2020) Gendered politics of memory and power: Making sense of Japan's peace constitution and the comfort women in East Asian international relations. *Analyses & Alternatives*, 4(2), 163–202 [in Japanese].

Dongwoo Lim is a Ph.D. student of Media and Journalism at the Graduate School of Interdisciplinary Information Studies, the University of Tokyo. His research at the University of Tokyo primarily focuses on analyzing social media through data analysis and solving social problems using computational social science methods.

Yuki Ogawa received his Dr. Eng. degree from the University of Electro-Communications, Japan, in 2011. He is currently a Lecturer at the Graduate School of Information Science and Engineering, Ritsumeikan University, Japan. He works on computational social science and social simulation.

Atsushi Tago is a Professor of International Relations at the School of Political Science and Economics, Waseda University. He received his Ph.D. from the University of Tokyo in 2007. He was a Professor at the Graduate School of Law, Kobe University by March 2018. He specializes in the scientific study of international politics. He has been a PRIO (Peace Research Institute Oslo) Global Fellow from 2017. He received the Japan Society for the Promotion of Science award in 2020.

Fujio Toriumi is a Professor at the Graduate School of Engineering, the University of Tokyo. He received his Ph.D. degree from the Tokyo Institute of Technology, Japan in 2004. His research interests are computational social science and artificial intelligence technologies for society.

Mitsuo Yoshida is an Associate Professor of Faculty of Business Sciences at the University of Tsukuba, Japan. He is also the founder of Tech-Tech Inc., which provides a news search engine and other services. He received his Ph.D. from the University of Tsukuba in 2014. His research interests are computational social science and the science of science.

1 Bringing people's voices back in Japan–South Korea relations

Yuki Asaba

Although Japan–South Korea (hereafter, Korea) relations have witnessed twists and turns over half a century since the normalization of diplomatic relations in 1965, the 2010s saw the most profound and far-reaching changes in the perceptions of Korea by Japanese people. Annual public opinion surveys on foreign affairs conducted by the Japanese Government Cabinet Office over recent decades showed significant changes in 2012[1], indicating that negative views of Korea among Japanese people, even "Korea fatigue," have now become the "new normal." In the latest survey in 2020, about two-thirds of Japanese people did not have "a feeling of friendship" with Korea, and over four-fifths appraised the current state of affairs in Japan–Korea relations as "not amicable." Both scores are overwhelming and persistent, and the latter is larger than the comparable figures for bilateral relations with China (81.8%) and Russia (73.9%) (Cabinet Office, the Government of Japan, 2021). As generally understood, Japan–Korea relations over the past decade have been the worst in either intertemporal or cross-national comparisons.

However, despite the general trend, there remain nuanced differences in Japanese people's perceptions of Korea between age-groups and sexes. The younger the respondents, the more favorable are their views of Korea. Only in the 18–29 age-group do the majority (54.5%) have a positive view of Korea (Figure 1.1). In a similar vein, women (42.5%) have more favorable opinions than men (27.0%) in relative terms, although the majority of both sexes have unfavorable opinions of the neighboring country.

Those differences provide a vivid illustration of Japanese experiences and understanding of matters related to Korea. For example, *Kim Jiyoung, Born 1982*, a book/movie about an ordinary Korean woman in her 30s struggling with her work–life balance in a male-dominated society and family is easily downloaded with Japanese translation. It is widely accepted by young Japanese women as typical of their own lives and is a common source of comfort and encouragement. Meanwhile, elderly men in Japan

DOI: 10.4324/9781003143536-1

2   *Yuki Asaba*

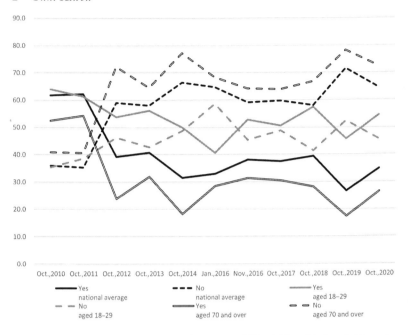

Figure 1.1 Changes in Japanese people's sense of friendship with South Korea by age-group in the 2010s.

Source: Cabinet Office, the Government of Japan (2021)

go to offline bookstores and find interesting and even consoling monthly magazines featuring "anti-Japanese" and "irrational" behaviors by Koreans in their entirety, ranging from President Moon Jae-in's annual speech on August 15 when Korea was liberated from Japan's colonial rule in 1945 to a number of rulings by the Korean supreme court and constitutional court concerning comfort women/sex slaves and forced labor/wartime workers.

Against this backdrop, it is all the more urgent to bring people back into the study of Japan–Korea relations, and especially different "voices" (Hirschman, 1970) in contrast with the manners in which past wrongdoings were "settled completely and finally" in diplomatic accords, historical animosity is linked with security and economic imperatives in the US–Japan–Korea triangle (Cha, 1999), and strategic visions of a future international order are shared/divergent in the context of the rise of China (Glosserman and Snyder, 2015).

This chapter addresses these questions by analyzing the increasing significance of public opinion in diplomacy. Part I provides an overview of major events in Japan–Korea relations in the 2010s. Part II sheds light on new actors in addition to governments in foreign affairs such as individuals, activist groups and movements, the media, and the judiciary. Finally,

Part III examines how Japanese people perceive these structural changes and define bilateral relations.

Part I. The state of affairs in Japan–Korea relations in the 2010s

It is striking that both the Japanese and Korean governments reached an agreement in December 2015 on one of the most contentious and long-simmering issues since Kim Hak-sun's first testimony on August 14, 1991 that she had been a comfort woman for the Japanese military during World War II. Unlike previous efforts at redress by the Japanese government, such as Chief Cabinet Secretary Yohei Kono's acknowledgment of the historical fact in 1993, letters of apology by prime ministers, and the Asian Women's Fund's "atonement" projects in the 1990s and 2000s (Kimura, 2019), the 2015 agreement was a joint endeavor by both the Japanese and Korean governments for "recovering the honor and dignity and healing the psychological wounds of all former comfort women" through their cooperation. For that purpose, Prime Minister Shinzo Abe expressed anew "his most sincere apologies and remorse" to them and contributed 1 billion yen (approximately 10 million dollars) from the state coffers to the Reconciliation and Healing Foundation (RHF), which the Korean government established the next year to offer 100 million won (approximately 100,000 dollars) for each surviving victim in any form whatever, be it reparation or compensation (Ministry of Foreign Affairs of Japan, 2015; Ministry of Foreign Affairs, Republic of Korea, 2015). This agreement was generally accepted by Japanese people with some conservatives questioning whether the issue had been "resolved finally and irreversibly" (Yomiuri Shimbun, 2016).

After the transition of presidential power in Korea in May 2017 from conservative Park Geun-hye to progressive Moon Jae-in, the Korean government unilaterally dissolved the RHF and virtually nullified the government-to-government agreement by characterizing it as lacking a victim-centered principle. In the meantime, 35 of the 47 survivors had accepted the money, even if they were not fully satisfied with the negotiation process or the terms of the agreement. The Korean government did not officially call for renegotiation, but both the Japanese government and people (not only the conservatives but average voters as well) concluded that Korea was an unreliable actor with which it was almost impossible and even meaningless to negotiate.

This distrust was further reinforced by a Korean lower court's epoch-making order in January 2021 that the Japanese government pay compensation to 12 comfort women by recognizing an exception to the principle of sovereign immunity under international law and the International Court of Justice. It was argued that the inhumane act committed by the Japanese government in organizing the comfort women system was a grave violation of *jus cogens*, or a peremptory norm of general international law from which states could not deviate in any way. Furthermore, the ruling concluded that individuals' claims were not waived by past diplomatic accords between Japan and Korea, whether the 2015 agreement or the 1965 treaty, which is in stark contrast to Japan's position that the issues were legally resolved and "no contention shall be made" (Article 2-3 of the 1965 treaty on claims) in any court.

Other rulings that shocked many Japanese were handed down by the Supreme Court of Korea (SCK) in October and November 2018, ordering Nippon Steel & Sumitomo Metal Corporation (renamed Nippon Steel later) and Mitsubishi Heavy Industry, respectively, to pay compensation to Koreans forced to work for them during World War II. The rulings were based on a (re)interpretation of the 1965 treaty whereby Japan and Korea concluded a normalization of diplomatic relations. The court found that mental harm and psychological injuries, setting aside unpaid salaries to those in forced labor, had not been covered in the treaty; so, individual claims to them were not waived. This innovative (re)interpretation paved the way for similar subsequent lawsuits against other Japanese companies that had been flatly rejected even by Korean courts before.

Not a single Japanese company in those cases has abided by the ruling; all have refused to pay compensation of about 100 million won (approximately 100,000 dollars) to each plaintiff. This contrasts with similar cases whereby some Japanese companies, such as Nishimatsu Construction, reached out-of-court settlements with Chinese "wartime workers" by recognizing past wrongdoings as such, expressing a sincere apology, and contributing a significant amount of money to the fund established to compensate them for their damages and injuries. The Japanese government maintains that Korean court decisions clearly violate the specific treaties and agreements between the two countries and the fundamental principle of *pacta sunt servanda* (agreements shall be binding) in general international law. Its position is simply that there is no room for another diplomatic negotiation and solution as long as Korea breaks its promises, as it did when the 2015 agreement on the comfort women issue was virtually nullified in the wake of a change of government and a domestic court's decision in favor of one of the parties.

An opinion poll shows that the vast majority of Japanese people firmly support the government's position on the forced labor/wartime workers issue, irrespective of respondents' sex, age-group, preferred political party, or (dis)approval of Prime Minister Shinzo Abe (December 2012–September 2020) (NHK, 2018; NHK, 2019; Yomiuri Shimbun, 2018). They also support future government retaliatory measures if Japanese company assets already seized by Korean authorities are liquidated. When such a unimodal and skewed distribution of public opinion occurs on any salient issue, it is generally risky for political leaders to take a different position from their followers.

The two abovementioned issues of comfort women/sex slaves and forced labor/wartime workers stem from Japan's colonial rule of the Korean Peninsula in 1910–45 and the postwar legal framework established after it ended. As Korea was not a party to the San Francisco Peace Treaty in 1951, in which its independence was recognized by Japan and "the Allied Powers waive all reparations claims of the Allied Powers, other claims of the Allied Powers and their nationals arising out of any actions taken by Japan and its nationals in the course of the prosecution of the war" (Article 14, paragraph (b)), "special arrangements" (Article 4, paragraph (a)) were made separately when Japan and Korea normalized their diplomatic relations in 1965. The provisions of the Japan–Korea claims treaty are that "the Contracting Parties confirm that [the] problem concerning property, rights and interests of the two Contracting Parties and their nationals (including juridical persons) and concerning claims between the Contracting Parties and their nationals … is settled completely and finally" (Article 2-1) and that "no contention shall be made with respect to the measures on property, rights and interests of either Contracting Party and its nationals" (Article 2-3).

Clearly, there exists a dispute between Japan and Korea concerning the interpretation and implementation of the 1965 claims treaty. On one hand, Japan (the government, Supreme Court, and average voters in general) maintains that individual claims were legally resolved by the treaty over half a century ago, and the Korean government should rectify its breaches of international law. On the other hand, Korean courts have ruled that such claims were not waived by the agreement between governments and justice should be done, even belatedly. So far, the Korean government has rejected the Japanese government's request that the dispute over the forced labor/wartime workers issue should be referred to arbitration by third parties as stipulated in the treaty. The Japanese government is also mulling the presentation of these cases to the International Court of Justice, whose compulsory jurisdiction Korea has not yet recognized, leaving almost no possibility of peaceful resolution through a legal process.

The dispute is underlain by the way in which Japan and Korea "agreed to disagree" on the terms of the 1965 treaty on basic relations, specifically the "already null and void" (Article II) clause regarding the lawfulness of Japan's 35-year colonial rule of the Korean Peninsula in 1910–45. While Japan maintained that it was lawful, if not morally justifiable, under the principle of intertemporal law at least until its surrender to the Allied Powers in 1945, Korea has insisted that it was null and void *ab initio*. Such "political prudence" or "collusion only among the elites" worked well for a few decades, but in the 2010s, "the 1965 system" was no longer a solid foundation for Japan–Korea relations but the point of greatest contention.

In the wake of the turmoil over the 1965 system, long years of diplomatic practice of preventing historical animosity from spreading into other realms of bilateral relations are now in crisis. In July 2019, the Japanese government suddenly tightened export procedures of some materials essential for the production of semiconductors and smartphones—Korea's major export items—apparently in retaliation for the Korean government's negligence concerning the issue of forced labor/wartime workers. In the following month, the Japanese government removed Korea from its whitelist of countries with preferential trade status, which antagonized Korean people and prompted a boycott of Japanese products. Sales of Uniqlo and Asahi Beer were severely hit, while those of Nintendo Switch and its GameSoft *Animal Crossing* had been rising steadily, especially during "stay home" periods of the COVID-19 pandemic in 2020. The Korean government also referred the case to the multilateral dispute settlement mechanism of the World Trade Organization (WTO). To many Koreans, Japan's actions on linking totally different historical and economic matters are unacceptable, as they are proud of their country finally becoming as powerful as Japan in terms of GDP per capita, while having a sense of victimhood and moral superiority concerning historical issues.

Security is no exception to such issue linkages. Immediately after Japan's imposition of export control/restriction measures, the Korean government threatened to terminate the General Security of Military Information Agreement (GSOMIA) with Japan, which was vitally important in addressing the ever-increasing threats from North Korea's nuclear and missile programs. Intelligence cooperation is not only mutually beneficial, but has implications beyond bilateral relations. Although Japan and Korea have not established a formal security alliance, they share a common ally, the United States, which expects them to work together closely. In the end, the Korean government backed down mere hours before the expiration of the security pact and put the WTO suit on hold as long as Japan remains sincerely engaged with policy consultation on the trade dispute. Such mutual distrust was already demonstrated in a serious incident in December 2018 when a Korean navy destroyer locked its fire-control radar onto a Japan Maritime Self-Defense Force P-1 patrol aircraft in the Sea of Japan/East Sea, although the Korean military denied it.

As every aspect of Japan–Korea relations remains in this state of affairs, the situation—to borrow an expression by Shin Kak-soo, former Korean ambassador to Japan from 2011 to 2013—is "a compound fracture unprecedented in the five decades" since the normalization of diplomatic relations in 1965 (Washington Post, 2019). If this diagnosis is correct, it is extremely difficult to perform surgery or prescribe medicine.

Part II. Different voices raised against the status quo

To comprehend the recent development of Japanese–Korean bilateral relations, we need to start with an overview of the roles and responsibilities of new actors in Japan–Korea relations other than elites in government, individuals, activist groups and movements, the media, and the judiciary. For example, Bae Chun-hee, Lee Chun-sik, and Yang Geum-deok, the plaintiffs in the legal cases against Japanese companies and government mentioned above in Part I, were the individuals most influential in bringing profound changes in bilateral relations in the 2010s. Previously unheard and silenced by their own government, courts, and neighbors, now they not only challenge the terms and practices of the previous intergovernmental agreements in 1965 and 2015 but also question what the government stands for and its responsibility and accountability to its citizens.

Another example of a different kind of individual increasing their presence in Japan–Korea relations is Makoto Sakurai, the founder of the ultranationalist, racist, and xenophobic grassroots social movement *Zaitokukai*, literally meaning "Association of Citizens Against Special Privileges for Korean Residents in Japan." Although its arguments are manipulated and totally groundless, the movement has to some extent succeeded in mobilizing fear and resentment of an ethnic minority among Japanese people in what was once believed to be a homogeneous society, and in triggering hate crimes in various forms such as against children at the Korean ethnic school in Kyoto. The perpetrators in the Kyoto case were prosecuted and duly punished, and some local municipalities later enacted more specific regulations on hate speech than the national law. Although Sakurai established the Japan First Party and ran in the Tokyo gubernatorial elections twice in 2016 and 2020 with 1.7% and 2.9% shares of the vote, respectively, far-right political parties have not flourished in Japan at either the national or local levels of government and parliament, unlike the Freedom Party of Austria, which participated in a coalition government in 2017–19.

Nevertheless, "Netto-uyoku" or those who post anti-Korean and anti-Chinese tweets or leave similar comments on Yahoo, the most popular portal site in Japan for daily news, are remarkably active and deserve serious research. Recent empirical studies by Fumiaki Taka (2015), Daisuke Tsuji (2017), and Naoto Higuchi (2016) show that such people remain few in terms of absolute numbers (at most, 1.8% of Japanese Internet users) and are not necessarily socioeconomically disadvantaged. It remains to be seen whether patterns of Internet use, especially social networking sites, and the left–right political divide and affective polarization are reinforcing each other in Japan. However, it is certain that individuals have now come to the fore both in domestic and foreign policies equipped with multiple news media and a variety of cognitive maps.

Annual opinion polls conducted jointly by Genron NPO in Japan and the East Asia Institute (EAI) in Korea since 2013 show that over 90% of both Japanese and Korean people rely on the domestic mass media (with television still predominant and news apps on smartphones becoming more popular, especially among young Koreans) for information on each other and Japan–Korea relations, given that four out of five Japanese and nine out of ten Koreans have no friends or acquaintances in the other country (Genron NPO, 2020; East Asia Institute, 2020). Less than one-fourth of citizens in either country believe that coverage of bilateral relations by domestic mass media is "objective and fair." At the same time, it is not true that they trust the Internet more than the mass media.

Before the Japanese product boycott and the outbreak of the COVID-19 pandemic, the number of Korean tourists visiting Japan had increased steadily since the early 2010s, reaching a historical peak in 2018 with 7.5 million (about one-seventh of the Korean population of 52 billion), who, together with people from mainland China, Taiwan, and Hong Kong, drove Japan's strategy of a "tourism nation" in the 21st century. In contrast, Japanese visitors (mainly female) to Korea have fluctuated in number during the past decade, only surpassing 3 million in three years: 2011, 2012, and 2019. Given the difference in population size between the two countries, the proportion of Japanese people with personal experience of visiting Korea and knowing people there is much lower than that of their Korean counterparts. Choi, Jeong, and Jung (2014) found in a one-shot 2011 survey that personal experiences of visiting Japan were not statistically significant in the positive attitudes of Koreans toward Japan, but it remains to be seen whether this result will be replicated in Korea one decade later in 2021, or in other settings in Japan.

One of the greatest difficulties in analyzing public opinion lies in the scarcity of available systematic and reliable data. Especially in the analysis of Japan–Korea relations, public opinion surveys on diplomacy have been conducted annually by the Japanese government since 1975, but no Korean equivalent exists, even in 2020. Only the same two questions (whether respondents feel a sense of friendship toward Korea and whether they regard Japan–Korea relations as amicable) were repeatedly asked over the decades, which makes it difficult to make a systematic intertemporal comparison. In this respect, annual opinion surveys in both countries by the Genron NPO and EAI since 2013 have been important, with basic questions retained over the past eight years, including personal attributes of the respondents such as sex, age, and school last attended. However, only the national average is made public, and no subsequent empirical research has been conducted. To make matters worse, as the previous decades of the 1990s and 2000s are concerned, the only available data are from the joint opinion polls sporadically conducted every few years with different sets of questions by sister newspapers in Japan and Korea, Asahi Shimbun and Donga Ilbo, Yomiuri Shimbun and Hankook Ilbo.

In addition to individuals, activist groups and movements, and the media, Korean courts and judges are another emerging and decisive actor in Japan–Korea relations, as illustrated by the controversial cases of comfort women/sex slaves and forced labor/wartime workers' issues. Generally speaking, diplomacy is a policy area with more discretion for the executive vis-à-vis other branches of government with the legislature left merely with the authority for *ex post* approvals, such as ratification of a treaty. Even within the executive branch, the Ministry of Foreign Affairs is sidelined in the process of foreign policy decision-making while the Prime Minister's Office (*Kantei* in Japan), the Presidential Office (the Blue House in Korea), or the core executive in general are becoming more influential based on trust by a top political leader, which is a global trend in recent years. As a nonelective organ, the judiciary tends to exercise self-restraint in making judgments on "political questions" in the constitutional system of checks and balances, leaving voters, or the sovereign people, a final say. Deciding on the constitutionality of a certain foreign policy or diplomatic agreements is one example of such self-restraint.

In this respect, the Constitutional Court of Korea (CCK), established in September 1988 for the first time in history in the wake of democratization and constitutional revision, is distinctly active in the judicial review of laws. In the 1987 Korean Constitution, individuals are also entitled to file a suit for act or omission of government in the CCK. For the past three decades from 1988 to 2018, the CCK has declared laws and acts or omissions of government unconstitutional or incompatible with the Constitution 2.5 times a week on average, which is appraised by Korean people as a manifestation of "transitional justice." As a guardian of the Constitution, the CCK is the most trusted actor among "We, the People of Korea" (Preamble of the Constitution), followed by the military, with other branches of government, political parties, and the media lagging far behind.

Treaties and agreements with Japan concluded by previous governments, especially during the authoritarian era, and diplomatic practices are now scrutinized by the CCK and its rival, the SCK. In August 2011, the CCK handed down a ground-breaking decision on the failure of the Korean government to resolve the comfort women issue as unconstitutional by upholding "the cause of the Provisional Republic of Korea Government born of the Independence Movement of 1 March 1919" (Preamble of the Constitution).

Thereby, it recognized a dispute with Japan concerning the lawfulness of Japan's 35-year colonial rule of the Korean Peninsula in 1910–45 and the interpretation and implementation of the "already null and void" provision (Article II) in the 1965 treaty on basic relations between Japan and Korea, concluded by President Park Chung-hee. The SCK's later rulings on forced labor are based on the same understanding of the Constitution and its relationship with international law, including bilateral treaties and agreements.

This judicial activism in Korea is perplexing to Japanese people living in completely different institutional settings wherein the Japanese Supreme Court, established in 1947 after the end of World War II, has declared only 10 legal provisions to be unconstitutional in more than seven decades. In the absence of a constitutional court, the Supreme Court and its 15 government-appointed judges have exercised self-restraint on political questions such as the constitutionality of the Japan–US security treaty, the basis of Japan's defense policy and national strategy. In postwar Japan, there have been no constitutional changes and only three changes of government: in 1993, 2009, and 2012. This political stability or inertia is in stark contrast with the dynamic relationship between politics, law, and justice in Korean constitutional history in which some retroactive applications of the law have occurred after revolutionary changes. For example, the Special Act on Asset Confiscation for Pro-Japanese and Anti-national Collaborators to the State enacted in 2005 was declared constitutional by the CCK six years later in the name of "transitional justice," albeit with the recognition of some elements of retroactive application of the law.

Although Japan and Korea are both consolidated democracies, vibrant market economies, and US allies in the Western Pacific by any international standard, their people do not have a sense of sharing the same political and economic systems. According to the joint opinion survey in 2020 conducted by Genron NPO and EAI, over half of the Japanese people regard Korea as a nationalistic country, while about 60% of Korean people deem Japan to be a militaristic power. For their part, the Japanese people wonder whether Korea is a trustworthy partner that shares "strategic interests and fundamental values" such as freedom, democracy, basic human rights, and rule of law. From 2015 on, Japanese government officials have ceased to use those expressions in describing Japan–Korea relations (Ministry of Foreign Affairs of Japan, 1971–2020).

Part III. Gaps in structural and perceptional changes

In the final part of the chapter, let me examine how Japanese people perceive the structural changes since the normalization of diplomatic relations in 1965. It is notable that Japan and Korea have differed significantly in recent years in relation to current threat perceptions and strategic visions for the future than in the accounts of the past.

In past decades, North Korea was undoubtedly the most significant and common threat to both countries as its nuclear and missile programs developed continuously. Especially after Kim Jong-un assumed power in December 2011, North Korea conducted nuclear tests four times and launched all types of ballistic missiles in order to strengthen deterrence: intercontinental (ICBM), intermediate-range (IRBM), medium-range (MRBM), and short-range (SRBM); ground-launched (GLBM) and submarine-launched (SLBM). It finally declared itself a nuclear power with the capability of targeting not only Guam, Seattle, and Los Angeles, but New York and Florida as well. Under the circumstances, policy coordination between Washington, Tokyo, and Seoul was, is, and will be desperately needed.

Threat is a function of an opponent's perceived intentions and capabilities. In this context, threat perceptions may be different even among allies, depending on their understanding of words conveying good intentions by a leader of the country with weapons of mass destruction and delivery systems, and with a track record of broken promises. One such perception gap is vividly illustrated by the controversy over the "complete denuclearization of the Korean Peninsula" in the Panmunjom Declaration of April 2018 issued by North and South Korea and in the Joint Statement of US President Donald Trump and the DPRK's (Democratic People's Republic of Korea, the North's official name) Chairman Kim Jong-un in a historic summit in Singapore in June 2018. For some, it means the "complete, verifiable, and irreversible denuclearization" (CVID) of North Korea. For others, this should be "simultaneously and in parallel" with corresponding measures by the US and the international community such as easing/lifting economic sanctions on North Korea imposed by United Nations Security Council resolutions, declaring an end to the 1950–53 Korean War, still technically continuing, and suspending/ scaling back regular military exercises between the US and Korea. Now that we are entering the 2020s with no meaningful progress either toward complete denuclearization of the Korean Peninsula, "new US–DPRK relations" or "a lasting and stable peace regime on the Korean Peninsula" (the Joint Statement in Singapore), perception gaps and miscalculations by all the relevant parties are apparent. Meanwhile, there have been changes of government or leadership from Republican Donald Trump to Democrat Joe Biden in the US and from Shinzo Abe through Yoshihide Suga to Fumio Kishida of the same Liberal Democratic Party in Japan. In Korea, a divide over the terms of denuclearization and the future of inter-Korean relations among the conservatives and the progressives has deepened under the Moon Jae-in presidency (May 2017–May 2022). The Japanese government and people are skeptical of President Moon's peace overtures to North Korea without defense readiness and close policy consultation with allies and neighbors.

This skeptical view of Korean diplomacy in Japan is no less manifest in relation to the rise of China and its challenges to the US-led postwar liberal international order based on rules and norms. A popular Japanese sentiment that Korea is tilting toward China was reinforced by a single picture of Korean President Park Geun-hye standing with Chinese President Xi Jinping and Russian President Vladimir Putin in Tiananmen Square in September 2015 to celebrate the 70th anniversary of the end of the Chinese People's War of Resistance against Japanese Aggression. One year previously, in a speech to Seoul National University students during his stay in Korea on a state visit, Chinese President Xi Jinping emphasized the common Chinese–Korean history of national humiliation by and joint resistance to Japanese imperialism in the 20th century and the incursions by Hideyoshi Toyotomi in the late 16th century. In this respect, President Moon's visit to the Provisional Republic of Korea (PRK) building in Chongqing in 2017 has implications beyond Chinese–Korean bilateral relations. The PRK was first established in Shanghai in the wake of the March 1 independence movement during Japan's colonial rule of Korea in 1919, and it moved around China several times with the help of the Chinese Nationalist Party—but neither the Communist Party nor the People's Liberation Army. In those accounts of the past, China's participation in the 1950–53 Korean War alongside the communist North was not officially raised even once.

Of course, there is no difference between Japan and Korea in the sense that China's presence is increasing in every aspect of the overall foreign relations of both countries. Especially in trade, China is the largest partner for both, surpassing the US in 2007 and 2003, respectively. However, its impacts are more consequential for Korea, as its economic growth overwhelmingly depends more on trade than on domestic consumption. Both the Japanese and Korean governments started using similar words to characterize their respective bilateral relations with China in the 2000s— "mutually beneficial relationship based on common strategic interests" and "strategic cooperative partnership"—but the meanings of "strategic interests/ strategic partner" for each country apparently differ in the late 2010s. It is in Japan's best national interests to strengthen the security alliance with the US, to pursue the idea of a "Free and Open Indo-Pacific" (FOIP), obviously a grand national strategy vis-à-vis China with the US, Australia, India, and other like-minded countries, and to maintain stable Japan–China relations simultaneously. It remains to be seen how Korea can strike a balance between the US and China as its strategic position in relation to FOIP is still ambiguous at best.

Those differences in the national strategy for the future of the international order are seen in a Japan–Korea joint opinion survey conducted by Genron NPO and EAI. In 2020, about one-third of the Korean people regarded China as the most important country in the world, in contrast with fewer than 10% of Japanese people. The majority of people in both countries (65.9% and 58.0%, respectively) still believe the US to be the most important partner in a period of global power transition.

Although to a lesser extent than the US–China hegemonic rivalry, Japan–Korea bilateral relations have experienced profound and far-reaching structural changes in the past few decades. At a time of normalization of diplomatic relations in 1965, power relations between the two were clear and asymmetrical. Japan's economic aid and technical support were vitally important for Korea's rapid economic growth and industrialization. When Japan joined the Group of Seven (G7) in 1975 as the sole Asian member, the Republic of Korea had neither a representative in the United Nations (in a joint accession with the DPRK in 1991, both were admitted as sovereign states) nor diplomatic relations with China and the Soviet Union (established in 1992 and 1990, respectively). During the cold-war period juxtaposed with authoritarian regimes until the late 1980s, the Korean government and people undeniably considered Japan a model for development and success.

For over 30 years from the 1990s through the 2010s, dubbed "the lost three decades" in Japan, power relations between the stagnant and rapidly aging Japan and dynamic Korea have become symmetrical. For example, as shown in Figure 1.2, GDP per capita PPP and annual military expenditure are now on par (World Bank; SIPRI).

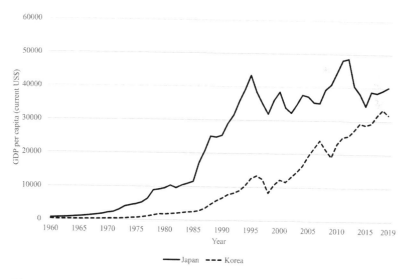

Figure 1.2 GDP per capita (current US$)—Japan and Korea.

Source: The World Bank https://data.worldbank.org/indicator/NY.GDP.PCAP.CD? locations=JP-KR

On the global stage, Korea joined the Organization for Economic Co-operation and Development (OECD) in 1996 and its Development Assistance Committee (DAC) in 2010, which was a great achievement for Koreans, who had once received foreign assistance and had now become a donor. Furthermore, Korea is an original member of the G20 with Japan and hosted the summit in Seoul in 2010. At an individual level, Korean students excel their Japanese rivals in TOEFL scores and English proficiency. Those feelings among Korean people of catching up with, being on an equal footing with, and even surpassing Japan culminated in a "K-quarantine" of national pride in response to the COVID-19 pandemic based on advanced information and communications technology, a transparent and accountable decision-making process, and a sense of solidarity among citizens. Japan is no longer a set point of reference for Korea, but rather one of the cases where success today is the seed of failure tomorrow in the current of the times.

In contrast, some Japanese people are perplexed at the completely changed historical and social reality of Japan–Korea relations and find it difficult to get along with Korea, seeing it as a tough competitor if not an enemy, or a colleague in areas of common interest. Perceptional changes can lag behind structural changes unless—so to speak—we continue to update our data and apps, and sometimes change the entire operating system of our hearts and minds. Against a backdrop of the gap between structural and perceptional changes, it is high time that Japanese people started asking what Korea—be it South, North, both Koreas or Korea as a whole—means for them at either the individual or collective level.

In this respect, Japan–Korea relations are a difficult case of the fundamental question of "peaceful change" in international relations. E.H. Carr (1939), a pioneering scholar of International Relations and a British diplomat, asserts that "the status quo" of both the domestic and international orders is always fragile and open to challenges of subversion such as revolution and war. This is because once sheer power relations at the time of state-building or the end of the war are built into legal and normative frameworks, it is difficult and almost impossible for "have-nots"—communists, women, defeated countries, and colonies—to make their voices heard in the existing political order so constituted, and to change it by the means available to them. The crisis is much more severe when changes in power relations after the establishment of those frameworks are not reflected in them, and a "revisionist" with increasing power tries to change "the status quo" using means other than peaceful elections, constitutional amendments, or treaty revision. In retrospect, Carr correctly anticipated Germany's displeasure with the status quo built in the Treaty of Versailles in 1919, which led to another world war and termed the "Twenty Years' Crisis" of the interwar period (1919–39) between the two most inhumane total wars in human history.

The treaties and agreements in 1965 clearly reflected not only the asymmetrical power relations between Japan and Korea but also the international norms and standards of the time. Although decolonization in Africa and Asia was underway in the 1960s, the lawfulness of colonial rule itself was never questioned in any other bilateral agreements between a former empire and a newly independent state. The 1965 system in Japan–Korea relations is within the inherent limits of the postwar settlement mechanism under the San Francisco Peace Treaty. Nevertheless, Japan has (to some extent) sincerely confronted the remaining postcolonial issues by supplementing/updating the 1965 system with another agreement with Korea: the 1998 Joint Declaration on Partnership. Japanese Prime Minister Keizo Obuchi expressed "deep remorse and heartfelt apology" for the "tremendous damage to suffering of the people of the Republic of Korea through its colonial rule" and Korean President Kim Dae-jung appreciated "the role that Japan has played for the peace and prosperity of the international community" in the postwar era. Carr argues that it is crucial to co-opt elements discontented with the existing order by meeting their demands for change to some extent. Otherwise, the status quo is abruptly challenged through unilateral action (Carr, 1939).

As Japan and Korea are in a crisis of representative democracy with a deepening political divide and affective polarization, their bilateral relations confront the problem of representation. Since the normalization of diplomatic relations in 1965, some people or issues have been overrepresented and others underrepresented. As we enter the 2020s, the distinction between high and low politics has become blurred, different voices are raised against malapportionment and gerrymandering in domestic elections, calling the "one person, one vote, one value" principle into question. In the same way, international relationships require "redistricting" to reflect significant demographic change proportionally, and such calls are clearly heard on every corner. Therefore, it is vital to bring people back to (studying) Japan–Korea relations and to make them duly counted at the ballot box, in an opinion poll, or through scientific research on public opinion, to which the remaining chapters of this book are dedicated.

Note

1 In August 2012, the following three events occurred within a one-month period. First, Lee Myung-bak landed on Takeshima/Dokdo, the islets over which Japan and Korea both claim territorial sovereignty, the first sitting South Korean (hereafter, Korean) President to do so. Second, President Lee demanded that the Japanese Emperor directly apologize for comfort women when he visits Korea in the future. Third, he flatly declared that Japan's national power had declined.

References

Albert O. Hirschman, *Exit, Voice, and Loyalty: Responses to Decline in Firms, Organizations, and States*, Cambridge, MA: Harvard University Press, 1970.

Brad Glosserman and Scott A. Snyder, *The Japan–South Korea Identity Clash: East Asian Security and the United States*, New York, NY: Columbia University Press, 2015.

Cabinet Office, the Government of Japan, "Gaikō ni kansuru Yoron Chōsa Reiwa 2-nen [Public Opinion Surveys on Foreign Affairs in 2020]," available on February 19, 2021. https://survey.gov-online.go.jp/r02/r02-gaiko/index.html

Daisuke Tsuji, "Keiryōchōsa kara miru Netto-uyoku no Purofairu: 2007 nen/2014 nen Uxebu Chōsa no Bunsekikekka o motoni [A Profile of Netto-uyoku: Quantitative Data Analysis of Online Questionnaire Surveys in 2007 and 2014]," Graduate School of Human Sciences, Osaka University, *Nenpō Ningen Kagaku [Annals of Human Sciences]*, 38 (2017), pp. 211–224.

East Asia Institute, "[The 9th Joint Korea-Japan Public Opinion Poll] Comparative Data," available on October 1, 2020. http://www.eai.or.kr/main/english/program_list01.asp?code=54

Edward Hallett Carr, *Twenty Years' Crisis, 1919–1939: An Introduction to the Study of International Relations*, London: Macmillan, 1939.

Fumiaki Taka, *Reishizumu o Kaibōsuru: Zainichi Korian eno Henken to Intānetto [The Anatomy of Racism: Prejudice against Zainichi Koreans in the Age of the Internet]*, Tokyo: Keiso Shobo, 2015.

Genron NPO, "South Korean attitudes toward Japan, have worsened dramatically, annual survey finds," available on October 19, 2020. https://www.genron-npo.net/en/opinion_polls/archives/5562.html

Jongho Choi, Han-Wool Jeong, and Heon Joo Jung, "Hangugin-ui dae-ilbon gamjeong-e michineun yoin-e daehan gyeongheomjeok bunseog: Ilbon-ui gun-sadaegughwa, gyeongjehyeoblyeog, keuligo jeongcheseong [An Empirical Study of South Korean Attitudes Toward Japan: Japan's Military Threat, Economic Cooperation and Identity]," Ilmin International Relations Institute, Korea University, *Kukche Kwan'gye Yŏn'gu [Journal of International Politics]*, 19: 1 (2014), pp. 41–76.

Kan Kimura (translated by Marie Speed), *The Burden of the Past: Problems of Historical Perception in Japan–South Korea Relations*, Ann Arbor, MI: University of Michigan Press, 2019.

Ministry of Foreign Affairs of Japan, "Announcement by Foreign Ministers of Japan and the Republic of Korea at the Joint Press Occasion," December 28, 2015. https://www.mofa.go.jp/a_o/na/kr/page4e_000364.html

Ministry of Foreign Affairs of Japan, "Diplomatic Bluebook," 1971–2020. https://www.mofa.go.jp/policy/other/bluebook/index.html

Ministry of Foreign Affairs, Republic of Korea, "Foreign Ministers of the ROK and Japan Meet Over the Issue of 'Comfort Women,'" December 28, 2015. http://www.mofa.go.kr/eng/brd/m_5674/view.do?seq=319622&srchFr=&srchTo=&srchWord=&srchTp=&multi_itm_seq=0&itm_seq_1=0&itm_seq_2=0&company_cd=&company_nm=&page=1

Naoto Higuchi (translated by Teresa Castelvetere), *Japan's Ultra-Right*, Tokyo: Trans Pacific Press, 2016.

NHK, "2018-nen 11-gatsu Seiji-ishiki Getsurei Chōsa [Monthly Public Opinion Surveys, November 2018]" November 2018. https://www.nhk.or.jp/senkyo/shijiritsu/pdf/aggregate/2018/y201811.pdf

NHK, "2019-nen 9-gatsu Seiji-ishiki Getsurei Chōsa [Public Opinion Surveys, September 2019]" September 2019. https://www.nhk.or.jp/senkyo/shijiritsu/pdf/aggregate/2019/y201909.pdf

Stockholm International Peace Research Institute (SIPRI), "SIPRI Military Expenditure Database" https://www.sipri.org/databases/milex

The World Bank, "World Bank Open Data" https://data.worldbank.org/

Victor Cha, *Alignment Despite Antagonism: The United States–Korea–Japan Security Triangle*, Stanford, CA: Stanford University Press, 1999.

Washington Post, "Japan–South Korea ties 'worst in five decades' as US leaves alliance untended," February 9, 2019. https://www.washingtonpost.com/world/asia_pacific/japan-south-korea-ties-worst-in-five-decades-as-us-leaves-alliance-untended/2019/02/08/f17230be-2ad8-11e9-906e-9d55b6451eb4_story.html

Yomiuri Shimbun, "Ianfu Goi 'hyōka' 49 pāsento [Results of Public Opinion Survey on Japan-Korea Agreement on Comfort Women Issue]," January 11, 2016.

Yomiuri Shimbun, "2018-nen 12-gatsu Denwa Zenkoku Yoron Chōsa [Monthly Public Opinion Surveys, December 2018]," jointly conducted with NNN (Nippon News Network), December 17, 2018. https://www.ntv.co.jp/yoron/tnvmcctideuawq3h.html

2 South Korea–Japan FCR crisis and public opinion

Gathering survey data in real-time crisis development

Shohei Doi, Kazunori Inamasu,
Shoko Kohama, Atsushi Tago

Introduction

From December 2018 to January 2019, South Korea (hereafter, Korea) and Japan were involved in repeated verbal fights over an incident related to their two navies. The Japanese government first claimed that a Korean destroyer had used fire-control radar (FCR) against one of the Japanese Maritime Self-Defense Force's patrol planes in open seas. As a reaction to this, the Korean government criticized the Japanese government for allowing its patrol plane to fly too low, thereby threatening the humanitarian rescue operation being conducted by the Korean destroyer. The two governments had initially agreed to deal with this incident in closed, working-level talks between defense ministry officials. However, they failed. Both governments ended up further denouncing each other in public statements, publicizing the recorded sounds of detected radar and even showing a short movie on their official websites. The contents of the evidence are contradictory and there is no objective way of determining who is telling the truth.

The two countries could have avoided repeated verbal fights over the incident; indeed, they initially tried to manage the incident through closed negotiations between the two governments. They had a choice of managing this incident through back channels, keeping it secret from their domestic publics. This would have allowed the two governments to save face and discuss how similar incidents could be discreetly handled in the future. In reality, however, the general public received negative information regarding each country throughout the first month of 2019. We can imagine how difficult it was for Japan and Korea, which share a common enemy (North Korea) and also share a common alliance partner (the United States of America) which wants the two countries to be closer for effective defense cooperation in East Asia (Asaba et al., 2020).

DOI: 10.4324/9781003143536-2

How do those verbal fights over an invisible crisis affect people's perceptions toward their own government and the opposition country? In a rare scientific research attempt by Kohama et al. (2017), it was suggested that messages denouncing the other side are more powerful in attracting political support from the general public than self-justifying statements or than not commenting at all. While this study is novel and important in helping us figure out how governments' messages are perceived by the general public in diplomatic quarrels (Rothschild & Shafranek, 2017), it was unfortunately weak in its external validity because the authors used a hypothetical case for their experiment.

In this study, we aim to reveal the consequences of actual verbal fights between Japan and Korea by utilizing three online surveys—right after the incident, a few weeks after the incident (but during oral fighting) and two months after the incident. We show how the cross-border verbal attacks over an invisible crisis affect people's perceptions of their own and the opponent's governments.[1]

Audience and invisible crises in international relations

In the audience cost argument in international relations (e.g., Fearon, 1994; Tomz, 2007), it is assumed that crises are basically public knowledge and are observed by a general audience (thus the public cares about what a leader would do in a crisis). However, many crises occur in isolated border zones or in open sea/air, where neither media nor third-party states/international organizations can confirm what exactly happened between the disputing countries. Crises are, in many cases, invisible to the general public. For instance, the lay public may not know how often the countries are involved in crisis situations, where and when such incidents happen, or what exactly occurs. Indeed, governments can hide some of the cases and efficiently manage incidents before letting their domestic audiences know about them (Kurizaki, 2007).

In such instances, the audience, in this case the general public, are usually only informed once the government makes a public statement, or at least leaks to the media, on the crisis incidents (Kohama et al., 2017). Governments can use official statements to make "denouncements" and "self-justifications," and inform their own domestic and third-party, international audiences that an incident had happened in a particular way. They can announce that the opposing side fired first or made the first provocative move (such as targeting a fire-radar to an unarmed patrol plane), and thus that their reaction even with material force was made only as a defensive measure; it may also be possible to categorically deny the opponent's claim over the incident; they could suggest the opponent's side is dishonest and is therefore lying.

People's perceptions toward such government statements are crucial when the invisible crises become visible and are recognized as a crisis situation. Do people believe what their own governments say without questioning their accuracy or do they cast doubt? While Kohama et al. (2017) assume that the people would not doubt the reliability of government information in an invisible crisis, this is something we should not simply *assume*. Government information in an invisible crisis may be critically assessed by the citizens and thus it may be seen as being untrue or at least doubtful. The weakness of Kohama et al. (2017) is the fact that they used a hypothetical crisis scenario, and thus their assumptions, findings, and implications may not hold in real cases. In particular, we wonder if people tend to perceive governmental information as true, which is somehow naively assumed in Kohama et al. (2017).

Given that the incidents could occur in areas where neither of the governments can be objective (each has the incentive to be seen stronger and more legitimate in their actions/claims) and no media can independently confirm the truth, people may have room to doubt what the government says in public statements over the crises. Who would believe what their government says in such an invisible crisis? Or, to put the question another way, how do people formulate their beliefs regarding an invisible crisis? These questions are important to ask in the context of the Korea and Japan relationship, where further invisible crises could easily, and perhaps frequently, occur in the near future; the general public reaction might heavily determine how the governments react to those incidents.

As mentioned in the *Introduction* of this chapter, on December 20, 2018, according to the Japanese explanation, a Korean Navy destroyer, ROKS Gwanggaeto the Great (DDH-971), directed its FCR at a Japanese SDF maritime patrol aircraft (Kawasaki P-1) that was conducting surveillance operations off the Noto Peninsula in the Sea of Japan at around 3 p.m., Japan Standard Time. The Ministry of Defense (MoD) of Japan claimed that directing FCR toward a plane is a violation of the Code for Unplanned Encounters at Sea (CUES), and stated that the act of locking with FCR is generally considered as a hostile act, one step short of actual firing. The Japanese MoD also claimed that the radar hit multiple times, and no response was made to communications from the Japanese aircraft by the Korean destroyer.

By contrast, Korea denied the Japanese claims a day after Japan made its accusation. According to statements by the Korean military, the destroyer did not use FCR but MW08 radar for the rescue operation. When the Japanese aircraft arrived at the site, it was participating in the rescue of a distressed North Korean fishing boat. Contradicting Japanese claims that the incident occurred off the coast of the Noto Peninsula, the Korean military claimed that the location of the incident was approximately 100 km northeast of the Liancourt Rocks.

From the final two weeks of December 2018 to the end of January 2019, the two governments were involved in repeated verbal fights over this incident: denouncements about the other side's unprofessional manners and/or overreaction; requests for a formal apology and promises to prevent similar incidents happening in future; and a variety of accusations of the other side as having unfriendly military forces while both are formal allies of the United States and share the same critical security threat (North Korea).

Our central questions here, then, are *how those incidents were seen by the general public* in Japan and *how the public formulate perceptions of the crisis, the two governments, and the bilateral relationship.*

Survey method

As this crisis developed over months, our team conducted three waves of surveys (note: while we use the term "wave," it was not a panel design and thus in each time, the respondents were fresh samples).

The first survey was performed in the last week of December 2018, that is, right after the first claim by the Japanese government regarding the FCR incident. It was conducted via an online crowd-sourcing company and used Qualtrics. The total number of participants was 1,716 (898 males and 709 females, 109 undeclared). The age of participants ranged from 18 to 69 years, with a mean age of 39.6 years ($SD = 11.6$). While conducting this first wave survey, we were able to exploit a natural experiment type of informational stimulus from the Japanese government: it disclosed a video taken by the SDF aircraft. We divided the sample of the first wave by before and after the video disclosure.

The second survey had an experimental setting in addition to the normal survey questions asked in the first wave and was then approved by the institutional review board of Kobe University (School of Law IRB, 30012). This survey experiment was created by using Qualtrics and conducted through Nikkei Research Inc. (http://www.nikkei-r.co.jp/english/), a nationally well-known survey firm in Japan. The total number of participants was 1,469 (659 males and 638 females, 172 undeclared). The age of the participants ranged from 21 to 69 years, with a mean age of 52.0 years ($SD = 14.1$).

The third, final survey was conducted in March 2018 using a system operated by Nikkei Research Inc. The total number of participants was 2,354

(1,150 males and 1,188 females, 16 undeclared). The age of the participants ranged from 22 to 66 years, with a mean age of 48.4 years (*SD* = 13.1).

In total, we have four different samples of those public opinion surveys—one from the first wave survey before the video disclosure (group 0); second from the first wave survey after the video disclosure (group 1); a second wave sample (group 2); and a third wave sample (group 3).[2]

Questions asked

In all surveys, the participants were asked if they thought the following sentences regarding the facts were correct: [Fact 1] the Korean destroyer used a fire-radar on an unarmed patrol plane; [Fact 2] the Korean destroyer was searching for a North Korean vessel; [Fact 3] the Japanese government strongly requested the Korean government to prevent an incident; [Fact 4] the Korean radar was used multiple times and in a continuous manner; [Fact 5] the Japanese Maritime Self-Defense Force plane was flying low over the Korean destroyer; [Fact 6] the Japanese Maritime Self-Defense Force plane called the Korean destroyer by radio; [Fact 7] the incident happened in the Japanese EEZ; [Fact 8] such use of radar was a final act before firing; [Fact 9] the Japanese Maritime Self-Defense Force plane was violating international law, [Fact 10] the incident happened in Korean territorial waters; and [Fact 11] the Japanese government requested the Korean government to apologize. The participants were asked to select from 1) true, 2) not true, and 3) do not know. These questions were chosen to determine how aware respondents were of the incident and their degree of support for a particular government's position. For instance, [2] and [5] are typical of claims by the Korean government, while [4] and [6] are typical of the Japanese claims. If a person is objective enough, they may not easily select either true or not true but choose do not know.

After the eleven questions, we asked five each (in total ten) questions on their attitudes toward the two governments, Japan and Korea: [Gov 1] whether they support the actions by the Japanese Maritime Self-Defense Force plane (support the actions by the destroyer of Korean Navy); [Gov 2] support the protest against the Korean government by the Japanese MoD (support the Korean statement that it would like to fully explain to prevent the misunderstanding), [Gov 3] believe that Prime Minister Abe's announcement regarding the incident was politically motivated (believe that President Moon's announcement regarding the incident was politically motivated), [Gov 4] believe the actions by the Japanese Maritime Self-Defense Force plane were legitimate (believe the actions by Korean Navy destroyer were legitimate), and [Gov 5] feel that Japanese government was hiding something (feel that Korean government was hiding something). The participants were asked to select from 1) disagree,

2) somewhat disagree, 3) neither agree nor disagree, 4) somewhat agree, 5) agree, and 6) do not like to answer.

Furthermore, we also asked nine questions on their attitudes toward potential policies that should have been taken by the two governments: [Policy 1] the incidents should not be open to the public and they should be solved discreetly by the diplomatic agencies; [Policy 2] the incidents should not be open to the public and they should be solved discreetly by the military forces; [Policy 3] the incidents should not be solved by the top leaders of the two countries; [Policy 4] Korea should have apologized; [Policy 5] Japan should have reacted in a restricted manner and should not denounce Korea; [Policy 6] Japan should have reconsidered its countermeasures and made Korea stop what it had been doing; [Policy 7] Japan should have asked a third party like the US government and the US armed forces to intervene; [Policy 8] Japan should have asked a third party like the UN to intervene; and [Policy 9] Japan should have shown clear evidence of Korean use of FCR. The participants were asked to select from 1) disagree, 2) somewhat disagree, 3) neither agree nor disagree, 4) somewhat agree, 5) agree, and 6) do not like to answer.

We also measured Conservatism; the participants self-rated their political attitude on an 11-point scale with two poles: 0 = "progressive" and 10 = "conservative," with 5 as a choice indicating "neutral." Japanese political scientists use the word "progressive (kakushin)" in place of "left (saha)" or "liberal (riberaru)" to measure ideology in Japan. We coded those answering 7–10 as being right-wing (337 people in the second wave sample)[3] and those answering 0–4 as left-wing (161 people in the second wave sample); since Japanese people tend to scale themselves to the conservative, we decided to include one scale more to the left-wing. Changes in the coding (such as 8–10 for the right-wing and 0–3 for the left-wing) did not change the outcome significantly from what we show in the later section.

To further measure the key psychological determinants that could affect attitudes toward international issues (Mifune et al., 2019), we included social dominance orientation (SDO) and militarism variables in the estimation. The SDO has recently been considered to be a key determinant of resistance to political apology and status-seeking behaviors/perceptions (e.g., Renshon, 2017; Ohtsubo et al., 2021). We used the Japanese version of SDO6 (Pratto et al., 1994, 2006) to measure participants' SDO. The scale comprises eight items pertaining to the endorsement of inequality among groups (e.g., "It's probably a good thing that certain groups are at the top, and other groups are at the bottom; inferior groups should stay in their place") and another eight items regarding the endorsement of equality among groups (e.g., "All groups should be given an equal chance in life; no one group should dominate in society"). The 16 items (after the latter eight item scores were reversed) were averaged to obtain a single

SDO score. To assess militarism, participants rated their level of support for the statement "in international politics, it is often necessary to use military power to protect national interests" on a four-point scale (1 = "strongly disagree" to 4 = "strongly agree").

In the surveys, we asked other questions regarding the ideal actions by the government in this situation and their political attitudes toward multiple foreign countries including Korea, and demographic information such as a location of residence, age, gender, and education level. An English translation of the full survey is available in the web appendix.[4]

To make a fair comparison of different groups, which were gathered at different times and used different settings (e.g., crowd-sourcing vs. survey firm and use of Qualtrics system and one by Nikkei Research), we used multiple balancing techniques. In particular, we used the Entropy Balancing: *ebal*; Coarsened Exact Matching: *cem*; and Covariate Balancing Propensity Score: *cbps* (Hainmueller, 2012; Iacus et al., 2012; Imai & Ratkovic, 2014).

For the balance test, Figure 2.1 provides information on the standardized biases among group pairs visualized by using the *BalanceR* (https://github.com/JaehyunSong/BalanceR). The zero standardized bias means the minimum difference of the compared groups. In social sciences, the score 25 is the usual threshold to judge the significant bias in the compared data. Group 1 is thus significantly different over *age* and shows some difference in the residential region (*Kanto*). After the application of the

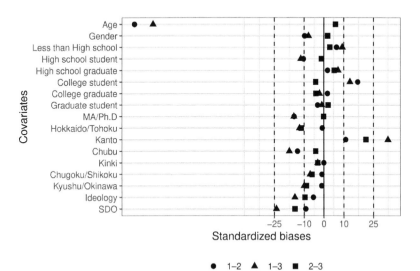

Figure 2.1 Covariate balance of three groups.

Note
1 is 1st wave; 2 is 2nd wave; 3 is 3rd wave

multiple balancing techniques, we could reduce the biases in most covariates, and they are thus roughly comparable even though the data collection was carried out in different settings.

Results

In this section, for the sake of limited space, we only show the results calculated after applying the Covariate Balancing Propensity Score technique (Imai & Ratkovic, 2014); for outputs using other balancing techniques, please see the appendix (Figures A1–A6). Figures 2.2, 2.3, and 2.4 show respondents' assessment of the facts regarding the incidents, evaluations

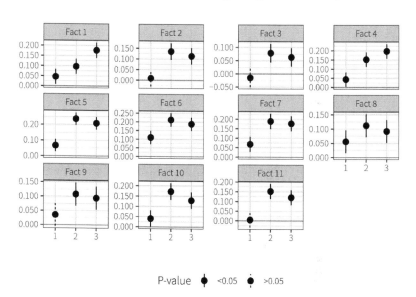

P-value ● <0.05 ● >0.05

Figure 2.2 Assessment of fact (covariate balancing propensity score).

Note
Baseline is group 0. The abbreviation of Fact # corresponds to the following statements:

Fact 1	ROK used a fire-radar to a patrol plane.	Fact 7	It happened in the Japanese EEZ.
Fact 2	ROK destroyer was searching an NK vessel.	Fact 8	The radar was an action right before firing.
Fact 3	Japan requested ROK to prevent an incident.	Fact 9	Japan was violating international law.
Fact 4	ROK radar was used multiple times.	Fact 10	It was in Korean territorial water.
Fact 5	Japanese plane was flying low.	Fact 11	Japan requested ROK to apologize.
Fact 6	Japanese plane used the radio.		

The bars indicate 95% confidence intervals.

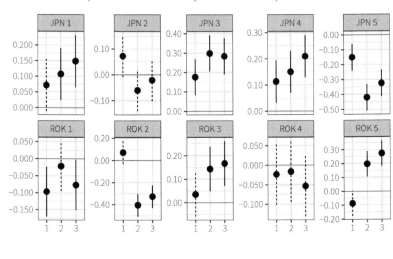

P-value ● <0.05 ● >0.05

Figure 2.3 Assessment of two governments (covariate balancing propensity score).

Note

Baseline is group 0. The abbreviation of JPN/ROK # corresponds to the following statements:

JPN/ROK 1	Support the actions by Japanese SDF/Support the actions by the ROK Navy.
JPN/ROK 2	Support the JPN protest against ROK/Support ROK statement to fully explain.
JPN/ROK 3	Feel the political motive of Abe/Feel the political motive of Moon.
JPN/ROK 4	Feel legitimacy about Japanese actions/Feel legitimacy about ROK actions.
JPN/ROK 5	Feel Japanese gov. is hiding something/Feel ROK gov. is hiding something.

The bars indicate 95% confidence intervals.

on the two governments, and potential policies that should be taken by the two governments.

On the fact-related questions, in Figure 2.2, we can see increasingly that the Japanese public had been more informed and held a particular view on what had happened in the Sea of Japan. In almost all of the panels, we see an increasing trend on the positive side; that is, respondents confirmed more that 1) the Korean destroyer used a fire-radar on an unarmed patrol plane, 2) the Korean destroyer was searching a North Korean vessel, 3) the Japanese government strongly requested its Korean counterpart to prevent an incident, 4) the Korean radar was used multiple times and in a continuous manner, 5) the Japanese Maritime Self-Defense Force plane was flying low over the Korean destroyer, 6) the Japanese Maritime Self-Defense Force plane was calling the Korean destroyer by the radio, 7) the incident happened in the Japanese EEZ, 8) the use of the radar was seen

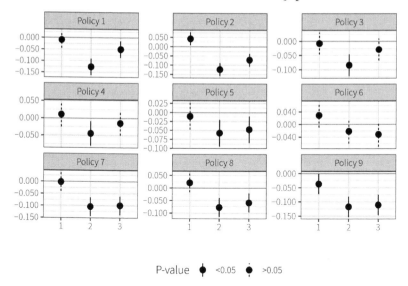

P-value ● <0.05 ● >0.05

Figure 2.4 Assessment of potential policies (covariate balancing propensity score).

Note
Baseline is group 0. The abbreviation of Policy # corresponds to the following statements:

Policy 1	Support discreetly solved among the diplomats.	Policy 6	Japan should have reconsidered its countermeasure.
Policy 2	Support discreetly solved among the military.	Policy 7	Japan should have asked the USA to intervene.
Policy 3	Support not solved by top leaders.	Policy 8	Japan should have asked the UN to intervene.
Policy 4	ROK should have apologized.	Policy 9	Japan should have shown clear evidence.
Policy 5	Japan should have reacted in a restricted manner.		

The bars indicate 95% confidence intervals.

as a final action before firing, 9) the Japanese Maritime Self-Defense Force plane was violating international law, 10) the incident happened in Korean territorial water, and 11) the Japanese government requested its Korean counterpart to apologize.[5]

As it is a typical case of an invisible crisis (Kohama et al., 2017), this increasing trend of confirming a particular piece of information on the event (in this specific case, biased toward the Japanese explanation on the event) suggests that the general public was exposed to a similar justification on what had happened in an open sea. Since we switched the survey platform between waves 1 and 2 from crowd-sourcing to Nikkei Research, it is important to note that the difference could also be due to the sampling method.

Moving to Figure 2.3, regarding questions on reactions and statements made by the Japanese and Korean governments during the crisis, we can see a variety of both positive and negative reactions to different questions at different times. As time passed, people tended to support the actions by the Japanese Maritime Self-Defense Force plane [JPN 1] and felt legitimacy about the actions by the Japanese Maritime Self-Defense Force plane [JPN 4]. Also, the more time passed, the more people came to believe there was a political motive driving Prime Minister Abe, who decided to uncover the incident; a similar change can be seen for the question regarding President Moon [JPN 3/ROK 3].

While the level of support for the protest against the Korean government by the Japanese MoD did not change, the level of support for the Korean statement that it would like to fully explain to prevent the misunderstanding did: it declined in waves 2 and 3. The level of distrust toward the Korean government increased as time passed. Finally, we see a clear contrast on the questions asking if they consider that the Japanese/Korean government is hiding something [Gov 5]. As time passed, Japanese people were getting more confident that their government was not hiding information but they were growing to believe that the opposite was true for the Korean government; in waves 2 and 3, the public considered more that the Korean government was hiding something.

Figure 2.4 shows the respondents' reactions toward the nine questions on their attitudes about potential policies that should have been taken by the two governments. In principle, the people tend to *disagree* with the questions being asked. Those include [Policy 1] the incidents should not be open to the public and discreetly solved among the diplomatic agencies, [Policy 2] the incidents should not be open to the public and discreetly solved among the military forces. As the crisis becomes a negative "war of words," the people lose rational judgment; as such, levels of support for a "behind-the-curtain" style of diplomatic solution diminishes.

Moreover, we see a similar disagreement with the questions like [Policy 3] the incidents should not be solved by the top leaders of the two countries, [Policy 4] Korea should have apologized, [Policy 5] Japan should have reacted in a restricted manner and should not denounce Korea, [Policy 7] Japan should have asked the third party like the US government and the US armed forces to intervene, [Policy 8] Japan should have asked a third party like the UN to intervene, and [Policy 9] Japan should have shown clear evidence of Korean use of FCR. We could not see such a time trend, except for in question 6 ([Policy 6] Japan should reconsider its countermeasures and make Korea stop what it had been doing).

Conclusion

Invisible crises inevitably end up with negative denouncement battles as long as a government wants to obtain their domestic support, especially from politically conservative people (Kohama et al., 2017). They trust their own government and distrust the opponent. This study gathered original data on a crisis between Japan and Korea in 2018–19. The evidence shows that as time passes, the general public confirms their information, in particular, something positive toward their own government (Japan) and negative toward the opponent government (Korea). Over the crisis, Japanese people tend to consider the Korean government as less trustworthy and hiding something. The more time passes, the more the people tend to believe what their own government says.

We believe that the general public's impression/image can be determined depending on how the general public is informed, or more precisely, "framed" about the incident and how this framing develops as time passes. Seeing more political intentions of the leaders and distrust of the government could lead to a conspiracy belief when there is uncertainty around the situation (van Prooijen & Jostmann, 2013). As van Prooijen et al. (2015) suggest, this type of conspiracy belief can be seen among holders of extreme political/ideological beliefs: more studies need to be made to better understand how an invisible crisis leads to an actual visible escalation of international disputes.

In concluding the article, how should we evaluate the overall effects of this type of invisible crisis on the already tense bilateral relations between Korea and Japan? Our data show that the crisis does indeed lead to a deterioration of the public's image of the opposing country; while we do not have survey data on the Korean side, we can easily imagine a similar tendency toward Japan and its government would exist in Korea as well. Given the easily provoked general public on both sides, one possible approach of the governments is to make such an incident as invisible and unnoticeable to the general public as possible. Back-channel communications between the governments could indeed prevent the general public from being heated up and accumulating negative feelings toward the other side.

More practically, discrete handling may be impossible since the open media can leak the information and the public may know what happened in open air or sea. If that is the case, we may expect third-party involvement. As Asaba et al. (2020) suggest in their study using American military-made videos, shared threat perception against North Korea (or another possible common enemy) and an emphasis on the fact that two countries are key American allies may drive a positive public perception toward the other side among Japanese and Koreans. As two East Asian democracies, the governments cannot function without obtaining a certain level of public support for their policies. While direct communication may not be well received by the other public, third-party information might have more credibility and may convey a message of cooperation, which may generate a positive view among the general public toward the other.

Notes

1 Even when a state is involved in an actual military crisis, verbal communication usually comes first, and what they say and do not say in their statements may determine how the crisis develops (e.g., McManus, 2015). In particular, among democracies, making an appropriate statement in a crisis can be a tough challenge. This is because, as the "audience cost theory" suggests, a democratic audience might punish its leader if s/he does not meet their expectations. For instance, if its own governments look weaker to the opponent, or if it indeed backs down, the general public may see their political leader as incapable of leading the country and their support for him/her may significantly decrease (Fearon, 1994; Tomz, 2007). Therefore, governments try to be seen as stronger and more capable against the opponent (CNN, 2019), and make public announcements that categorically deny the other's acts and deeds, and warn the opponent government to back down. Such a "strong" announcement could escalate a crisis or, at least, freeze the bilateral relationship as a conflicting one.

2 In the second and third waves, as an experimental treatment, we used a short paragraph to remind the participants that the incident was an invisible crisis and even the government could not know what exactly happened in the frontline. The control group did not receive such a paragraph. In this study, we do not report the experiment's findings due to limitations of space. We considered that the reminder of the invisible nature of the incident might affect people's perceptions toward the two countries' official announcements and process information more cautiously. The funding for these studies was provided by JSPS Kakenhi [15KT0053; 17H00973; 18KK0040].

3 We asked the question in all three waves.

4 https://github.com/A-Tago/replication-data-for-Korea-Japan-FCR-Crisis-and-Public-Opinion-/find/main

5 We admit that there is a logical contradiction for the affirmative answers to both questions 7 and 10 since if it had happened in the Japanese EEZ, it would not be within the ROK's territorial waters. However, it is possible that those legal jargons may not well be understood by the general public (and thus they did not notice the inconsistency), and they answered "yes" to any technical question if they were asked, especially when time passed.

References

Asaba, Yuki, Kyu S. Hahn, Jang Seulgi, Tetsuro Kobayashi, and Atsushi Tago (2020). "38 seconds above the 38th parallel: How short video clips produced by the US military can promote alignment despite antagonism between Japan and Korea," *International Relations of the Asia-Pacific*. 20(2): 253–273.

CNN (2019). "Why being seen as tough on Pakistan helps India's Modi" (February 27, 2019). https://edition-m.cnn.com/2019/02/26/india/india-pakistan-kashmir-analysis-intl/index.html

Fearon, James D. (1994). "Domestic Political Audiences and the Escalation of International Dispute," *American Political Science Review*. 88(3): 577–592.

Hainmueller, Jens (2012). "Entropy balancing for causal effects: A multivariate reweighting method to produce balanced samples in observational studies," *Political Analysis*. 20(1): 25–46.

Iacus, Stefano M., Gary King, and Giuseppe Porro (2012). "Causal inference without balance checking: Coarsened exact matching," *Political Analysis*. 20(1): 1–24.

Imai, Kosuke, and Marc Ratkovic (2014). "Covariate balancing propensity score," *Journal of the Royal Statistical Society: Series B (Statistical Methodology)*. 76(1): 243–263.

Kohama, Shoko, Kazunori Inamasu, and Atsushi Tago (2017). "To Denounce, or Not To Denounce: Survey Experiments on Diplomatic Quarrels," *Political Communication*. 34(2): 243–260.

Kurizaki, Shuhei (2007). "Efficient Secrecy: Public versus Private Threats in Crisis Diplomacy," *American Political Science Review*. 101(3): 543–558.

McManus, Roseanne W. (2015). *Statements of Resolve: Achieving Coercive Credibility in International Conflict*. New York, NY: Cambridge University Press.

Mifune, Nobuhiro, Kazunori Inamasu, Shoko Kohama, Yohsuke Ohtsubo, and Atsushi Tago (2019). "Social dominance orientation as an obstacle to intergroup apology," *PLOS ONE*. 14(1): e0211379. DOI: 10.1371/journal.pone.0211379

Ohtsubo, Yohsuke, Kazunori Inamasu, Shoko Kohama, Nobuhiro Mifune, and Atsushi Tago (2021). "Resistance to the six elements of political apologies: Who opposes which elements?" *Peace and Conflict: Journal of Peace Psychology*. 27(3): 449–458.

Pratto, Felicia, James Sidanius, Lisa M. Stallworth, and Bertram F. Malle (1994). "Social dominance orientation: A personality variable predicting social and political attitudes," *Journal of Personal Social Psychology*. 67(4): 741–763.

Pratto, Felicia, James Sidanius, and Shana Levin (2006). "Social dominance theory and the dynamics of intergroup relations: Taking stock and looking forward," *European Review of Social Psychology*. 17: 271–320.

Renshon, Jonathan (2017). *Fighting for Status: Hierarchy and Conflict in World Politics*. New York, NY: Princeton University Press.

Rothschild, Jacob E., and Richard M. Shafranek (2017). "Advances and Opportunities in the Study of Political Communication, Foreign Policy, and Public Opinion," *Political Communication*. 34(4): 634–643.

Tomz, Michael (2007). "Domestic Audience Costs in International Relations: An Experimental Approach," *International Organization*. 61(4): 821–840.

van Prooijen, Jan-Willem, and Nils B. Jostmann (2013). "Belief in conspiracy theories: The influence of uncertainty and perceived morality," *European Journal of Social Psychology*. 43: 109–115.

van Prooijen, Jan-Willem, André P. M. Krouwel, and Thomas V. Pollet (2015). "Political Extremism Predicts Belief in Conspiracy Theories," *Social Psychological and Personality Science*. 6(5): 570–578.

3 When will Japan's apology lead to reconciliation with South Korea?

Tetsuro Kobayashi, Atsushi Tago,
Kyu S. Hahn, Yuki Asaba

Since the 1990s, the issue of comfort women, women who were sexually enslaved by the Japanese military during World War II, has been a primary conflictive one between Japan and the Republic of Korea. Although comfort women also included Chinese, Taiwanese, Filipino, Japanese, and European (e.g., Dutch) women captured during Japan's invasion of the Southeast Asian colonial territories, Korean comfort women have been the most salient historical issue between Japan and other victim countries. In 1991, Kim Hak-sun—a former enslaved comfort woman—publicly disclosed her experiences, and since that time, the issue has triggered several bitter conflicts between Japan and South Korea (hereafter, Korea), with some resulting in apologies from Japanese political leaders.

In January of 1992, in response to the increasing salience of the issue, Prime Minister Kiichi Miyazawa expressed "sincere remorse and apology for Japanese past actions which inflicted unbearable suffering and sorrow on the people of the Korean Peninsula," which was echoed by an apology by Chief Cabinet Secretary Koichi Kato in July of 1992. In 1993, the so-called Kono statement, an apology admitting that the Japanese military was involved in the recruitment of Korean comfort women, was issued by Chief Cabinet Secretary Yohei Kono. Japan was reluctant to make national reparations to former comfort women from the legal standpoint that the issue of reparations was settled completely and finally in the 1965 Agreement on the Settlement of Problems Concerning Property and Claims and on Economic Cooperation between Japan and the Republic of Korea; thus, it instead established the Asian Women's Fund to provide financial reparations, as well as medical and welfare services, to the women who had been victimized. In addition, four prime ministers sent letters to former comfort women expressing "deep remorse and heartfelt apology." However, the issue was framed in Korea as an egregious violation of women's rights, and thus, they actively sought recognition of the issue from the international community. Throughout this process, public opinion in Korea was unanimously

DOI: 10.4324/9781003143536-3

critical of Japan and a sincere apology, which many believed would serve as a bedrock for reconciliation, was consistently demanded.

The critical turning point came at the end of 2015. The foreign ministers of Japan and Korea met on December 28, 2015, and confirmed that the issue of comfort women had finally and irreversibly been resolved. In his statement, Prime Minister Abe expressed anew his most "sincere apologies and remorse" to all the women who underwent immeasurable and painful experiences and suffered incurable physical and psychological wounds as comfort women. Japan and Korea also agreed that the South Korean (hereafter, Korean) government would establish a foundation (later to be called the Reconciliation and Healing Foundation), to which Japan provided one billion yen from state coffers to provide financial aid to former comfort women and their families. Although the 2015 agreement was initially welcomed, at least by the Japanese public, the new Korean President Moon Jae-in, who took office in 2017, criticized the process in which the agreement was made for not taking a "victim-centered approach." In the end, the Reconciliation and Healing Foundation was dissolved in November 2018, a move protested by the Japanese government. Regarding the apology, in an interview with *The Washington Post* in June 2017, President Moon said that the point of resolving the issue was for "the Japanese government to take legal responsibility for its actions and apologize publicly."

These strenuous processes have led to remarkable disagreement in Japanese and Korean public opinion regarding the need for further apologies. According to joint surveys by *Yomiuri Shimbun* and the *Hankook Ilbo* in June 2019, 80% of Japanese people thought that Japan did not need to apologize further regarding the issue of comfort women, compared with 11% who thought that they should. By contrast, only 11% of Koreans thought that Japan did not need to apologize further, compared with 87% who thought that they should. This stark contrast between public opinion in Japan and Korea regarding the need for further apologies illustrates how difficult it has been for interstate apologies to lead to reconciliation.

On the Japanese side, many people feel so-called apology fatigue—the sense that although Japan has repeatedly apologized to Korea, these apologies have not been accepted (e.g., Kitagawa & Chu, 2021; Mifune et al., 2019). Apology fatigue causes the Japanese people to feel that apologizing does not make any difference, leading to a sense of resignation. Apology fatigue also subtly resonated in Prime Minister Abe's statement on the 70th anniversary of the end of World War II on August 14, 2015, four months before the Japan–Korea agreement on comfort women: "[w]e must not let our children, grandchildren, and even further generations to come, who have nothing to do with that war, be predestined to apologize."

This sense of helplessness was aggravated further by the 2018 Japan–Korea radar lock-on dispute in which a vessel of the Republic of Korea Navy (Korean) locked onto an aircraft belonging to the Japan Maritime Self-Defense Force, leading to the understanding that Japan and South Korea cannot cooperate on issues even as fundamental as security.

On the other hand, from the perspective of Korea, the issue of comfort women has not been wholly resolved because the victimized women were not involved in the process leading to the 2015 agreement. In addition, even when Japanese politicians have expressed "deep remorse and heartfelt apology," other politicians have often made revisionist remarks, calling the sincerity of Japan's apologies into question. Based on these understandings, many Korean people believe that the Japanese Prime Minister and/ or Emperor should meet victims in person and apologize directly. For example, although he later apologized, the speaker of the Korean National Assembly stated in February 2019 that the Japanese Emperor should apologize to former comfort women to resolve the wartime issue. Yet another domestic issue in Korea is the decision by the Constitutional Court in 2011 that ruled the Korean government's inaction on the issue of comfort women to be unconstitutional. Since this decision, Korean governments have intensified their criticism of Japan over the issue.

All of these different understandings about the issue of comfort women and the associated apologies made by Japan are vividly manifested in stark contrast in perceptions of the apologies. A comparative survey experiment described in this chapter asks whether some statements regarding the Japan–Korea relationship are "objectively correct or wrong." One factually correct statement was "[a]mong the successive prime ministers of Japan, none has expressed regret or apologized for past colonial rule and invasion by Japan." Among Korean respondents, 45% believed this statement to be correct, compared with only 13% of Japanese respondents[1]. Another factually correct statement, "[s]uccessive prime ministers of Japan have sent apologetic letters to former comfort women through the Asian Women's Fund," was endorsed by 24% of Japanese, but only 6% of Koreans.

Why have Japan's apologies not led to reconciliation between Japan and Korea over the issue of comfort women? What conditions would lead to forgiveness by the people of Korea? This chapter tackles these questions by conducting a cross-national experiment in Japan and Korea.

Ineffective intergroup apology

The social psychology literature consistently indicates that intergroup apologies rarely lead to forgiveness (Hornsey & Wohl, 2013; Philpot & Hornsey, 2008; Wohl, Matheson, Branscombe, & Anisman, 2013). There are several reasons why intergroup apologies are rarely effective. First, due to motivated reasoning, those who are motivated to maintain a positive image of their ingroup, especially a victimized group image, tend to resist accepting intergroup apologies. For example, although Japan made an official apology to Australia for its actions against Australian prisoners of war (POW) during World War II, a limited number of people remember the event (Philpot & Hornsey, 2011). Those with a strong Australian national identity tend to think that Japan never apologized. Intergroup apologies become even less effective when the victim group is motivated to retain victimhood status, which helps maintain collective identity (Buruma, 1999).

Second, even when intergroup apologies enhance forgiveness, the effect is rather ephemeral (Wohl, Matheson, Branscombe, & Anisman, 2013). While the perpetrator group tends to think the apology should be sufficient for reconciliation, the victim group tends to believe the apology is just an initial step in reconciliation, and thinks more of the acts and changes by the perpetrator group that follow the apology, resulting in short-lived effects of one-off apologies on forgiveness. When the perceived liability of the perpetrator group is grave, the perceived sincerity of the apology becomes even more important, and the long-term consequences of the apology are critically monitored by the victim group. Thus, even if each apology itself was based on good intentions, it is difficult to satisfy the victim group fully.

Third, intergroup apologies are hard to generalize as a whole to the perpetrator group. Philpot and Hornsey (2008) tested the effect of an apology by a former Japanese soldier for the actions of Japan and its military personnel that caused a high mortality rate among Australian POW in World War II. They found that the Australian participants tended to forgive the soldier who made the apology, but the effect did not generalize to Japanese people as a whole.

Fourth, it is known that the victim group tends to overestimate the effect of an apology on themselves. De Cremer, Pillutla, and Folmer (2010) found that the value of an imagined apology by a perpetrator is larger than that of the actual apology because humans are poor predictors of their own future affect and behavior. Because of this bias, the victim group tends to overestimate the effect of the intergroup apology before it is made. However, because the perceived value of the realized apology is lower than they imagined, the impact of the apology tends to be limited, or even negative (De Cremer, van Dijk, & Pillutla, 2010; Skarlicki, Folger, & Gee, 2004).

There are additional reasons why intergroup apologies have limited effects. For instance, Okimoto, Wenzel, and Hornsey (2015) point to normative dilution. That is, when the victim group perceives that political apologies have become more normative in recent years, it strengthens its tendency to ask for an apology and becomes less likely to offer forgiveness in response to an apology. This effect occurs because the perceived sincerity of the apology is diminished as a result of normative dilution. This is a dilemma in which the symbolic value of an apology is reduced when the act becomes normative and prevalent. Wohl, Hornsey, and Bennett (2012) point to the effect of infrahumanization, which refers to the biased perception that the ingroup is more capable than the outgroup of feeling secondary emotions such as remorse and guilt. Therefore, when the perpetrator group (i.e., the outgroup) apologizes using words describing secondary emotions, the members of the victim group tend to underestimate their sincerity, inferring that the perpetrator group is less capable of feeling the secondary emotions. As a result, apologies referring to secondary emotions not only backfire, but also elicit less forgiveness than those using words of primary emotions (e.g., sadness).

All of these mechanisms limit the effect of intergroup apologies on forgiveness. But what happens to the perpetrator group when their apology is not accepted? When a perpetrator group learns that their apology was not accepted, it reinforces prejudice against the victim group and attenuates their willingness to move forward with the reconciliation process (Harth, Hornsey, & Barlow, 2011). Therefore, the unaccepted apology undermines the motivations of the perpetrator group to engage in future reconciliation, making it even more difficult to ameliorate the already strained intergroup relationship. In summary, intergroup apologies only have a tenuous link with intergroup forgiveness (Hornsey & Wohl, 2013; Hornsey, Wohl, & Philpot, 2015; Wohl, Hornsey, & Philpot, 2011). Nevertheless, intergroup apologies, especially interstate political apologies, are becoming more normative and common. If intergroup apologies are likely to have a limited impact, why do we still observe modern states offering and demanding apologies?

The public nature of interstate apologies

Within the field of international relations and East Asia regional studies, several prominent studies on interstate apologies have been carried out (Lind, 2008, 2009), some specifically focused on Japan's apologies to Korea (Dudden, 2008; Iokibe, Komiya, Hosoya, & Miyagi, 2020; Kim, 2016; Kimura, 2019). Here, we do not review these studies extensively as they are primarily focused on the bilateral relations between Japan and Korea. Instead, our research questions focus on the public nature of intergroup apologies in which a prominent third party is involved.

The prominent difference between interpersonal and intergroup apologies is whether they are made in public (Wohl, Hornsey, & Philpot, 2011). While many interpersonal apologies are made in private, with only the perpetrators and victims present, intergroup apologies, especially those made between governments, are essentially public in nature. Apologies between states become international news heeded by not only governments, but also the third-party publics of other countries. These third parties are known to have negative impressions of victim groups who do not accept public apologies from perpetrator groups (Bennett & Dewberry, 1994; Risen & Gilovich, 2007). This negative impression of the "unforgiving victims" is so robust that it is observed even when the apology is clearly insincere.

These intricate dynamics involving third parties create competing motivations for both victim and perpetrator groups. For the victim group, unforgiveness can reflect a sense of entitlement: a belief in one's moral superiority, right to special privileges, and claim to large reparations for moral debts (Exline et al., 2004). Unforgiveness can also reflect a fear of being taken advantage of or of letting the offending group off too easily (Exline & Baumeister, 2000; Lazare, 2004). However, the reputation of the victim group will be tarnished if it continues to refuse public apologies from the perpetrator group. Regarding the perpetrator group, although their unaccepted apologies may induce prejudice against the victim group and attenuate their willingness to engage in the reconciliation process, these public apologies can appeal to the third parties, among whom they gain a positive impression.

This public nature of intergroup apologies has not been elaborated on within the social psychological literature, which focuses primarily on bilateral interpersonal and intergroup relations. When considering the impressions of third parties, it is plausible that perpetrator groups are incentivized to apologize, even when they anticipate that their apology is not likely to lead to forgiveness from the victim group. Likewise, the victim group may unwillingly accept the apology even when its perceived sincerity is low because they fear third parties' images of them as unforgiving victims. This is particularly the case in the context of international politics, where strategic self-presentation (i.e., impression manipulation) is even more crucial than in interpersonal or small group contexts.

In the context of Japan–Korea relations, the United States (US) is the most important third party because it is allied with both Japan and Korea. Although Japan and Korea do not have an official military alliance, the US, Japan, and Korea constitute a triangulated security cooperative (Cha, 1999), especially in the face of threats from North Korea. In fact, the realization of the 2015 pact between Japan and Korea, despite the lingering conflict over the issue of comfort women, was strongly pushed by the US, which feared that it would become a wedge issue between Japan and Korea at a time when the three countries needed to cope with the threat of North Korea (Cha & Kang, 2018). Given these historic and theoretical backgrounds, we ask the following research question:

> RQ1: Will US support for the position of Japan over the issue of comfort women enhance forgiveness among the Korean public?

In addition to RQ1, we test the effect of the perceived position of the third party on the members of the perpetrator group. Intergroup apologies have been studied primarily in the context of their effects on the victim group; thus, their effects on the perpetrator group have yet to be investigated. A notable exception is the "unaccepted apologies" study described above (Harth, Hornsey, & Barlow, 2011). However, it is important to study the effects on the perpetrator group because doing so will allow us to explore the motivation of the perpetrator to apologize even when their apology is rarely accepted. Therefore, we also ask a second research question:

> RQ2: What are the effects of Japan's apology to Korea on Japanese public opinion?

Method

We fielded a cross-national experiment in Japan (February 2017) and Korea (June 2017). Japanese data (N=1,298) were collected from CrowdWorks, a crowdsourcing platform similar to Amazon Mechanical Turk, while Korean data (N=1,300) were collected from the online panel of MacroMill Embrain, a leading online survey firm in Korea. In both countries, the target age range was 20–59 years. Quota sampling was employed when collecting the Korean data so that the marginal distributions of sex, age, and residential areas became comparable to those of the general population. The sample characteristics are summarized in Table 3.1.

The experimental procedures were identical in Japan and Korea. First, pretreatment covariates such as demographic variables and political attitudes were measured. The participants were then randomly assigned to one of four experimental treatment groups or a control group. The participants in each group read different descriptions of Japan's apology about the issue of comfort women (described below). After reading the respective descriptions, outcome variables were measured. After measuring the outcome variables, an Implicit Association Test was conducted to gauge

Table 3.1 Sample characteristics

		Japan	Korea
Sex (% female)		49.54	50.00
Mean age (range: 20–59 years)		36.27	39.39
Education (three levels: 0–1)		0.70	0.77
Ideology (conservative: 0–1)		0.54	0.46
LDP (Liberal Democratic Party) supporter		0.48	
DPK (Democratic Party of Korea) supporter			0.49
Independent		0.29	0.13
Feeling thermometer (0–1)	Japan	0.62	0.36
	Japanese people	0.72	0.44
	Korea	0.25	0.68
	Korean people	0.34	0.62

the implicit prejudice between participants in Japan and Korea, though analysis of those data is beyond the scope of this chapter.

Those assigned to the control group did not read any texts about the comfort women or Japan's apology on the issue. The statement-only group read the following baseline description of Prime Minister Abe's apologetic statements on the issue of comfort women:

> Foreign ministers of Japan and South Korea had a meeting on December 28, 2015 and confirmed that the issue of comfort women was resolved, finally and irreversibly. In the statement, Prime Minister Abe expressed anew his most sincere apologies and remorse to all the women who underwent immeasurable and painful experiences and suffered incurable physical and psychological wounds as comfort women.
>
> Prior to this pact, on the 70th Anniversary of the end of World War II, a statement by Prime Minister Abe, which was issued on August 14th, 2015, mentioned the issue of comfort women as follows: "We must never forget that there were women behind the battlefields whose honour and dignity were severely injured" and "We will engrave in our hearts the past, when the dignity and honour of many women were severely injured during wars in the 20th century". Furthermore, he apologized as follows: "Japan has repeatedly expressed feelings of deep remorse and heartfelt apology for its actions during the war. (...) Such position articulated by the previous cabinets will remain unshakable into the future".

Comparison of the control and statement-only groups constitutes a replication of previous studies that tested the effectiveness of intergroup apologies on forgiveness. For each of the other three treatment groups, one of three descriptions of the US position was added:

US supports Japan

> To Abe's statement on the 70th anniversary of World War II, the US government issued the statement below, through the National Security Council: "We welcome Prime Minister Abe's expression of deep remorse for the suffering caused by Japan during the World War II era, as well as his commitment to uphold past Japanese government statements on history" and highly evaluated postwar Japan as it "stands as a model for nations everywhere".

US supports Korea

> United States House of Representatives House Resolution 121 was passed in 2007, which requested that the Japanese government make an apology to former comfort women. President Obama said that the comfort women issue was "a terrible, egregious violation of human rights" at a joint press conference after meeting with South Korean President Park Geun-hye in 2014.

US supports Japan–Korea pact

> The US government issued a statement as follows: "We welcome today's announcement by the Governments of Japan and the Republic of Korea that they have reached an agreement regarding the sensitive historical legacy issue of 'comfort women'". It added, "We applaud the leaders of Japan and the Republic of Korea for having the courage and vision to reach this agreement, and we call on the international community to support it".

The "US supports Japan" description implies that the US is supporting the Japanese position, whereas the "US supports Korea" description implies that the US supports the Korean position in condemning Japan's atrocities. The "US supports Japan–Korea pact" description indicates US support for both Japan and Korea for their agreement on the 2015 pact. Note that all these descriptions are fact-based and thus preclude deception. These treatments were intended to manipulate the perceived position of the US, the most important third party in the context of the Japan–Korea conflict over the issue of comfort women.

As outcome variables, we measured willingness to forgive (Wohl & Branscombe, 2005) and attitudes regarding the issue of comfort women.

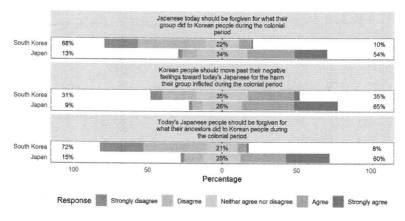

Figure 3.1 Distributions of willingness to forgive between Korea and Japan.

The willingness to forgive scale was composed of the following three items: "Japanese today should be forgiven for what their group did to Korean people during the colonial period," "Korean people should move past their negative feelings toward today's Japanese for the harm their group inflicted during the colonial period," and "Today's Japanese people should be forgiven for what their ancestors did to Korean people during the colonial period." These three items were measured with response options on a five-point scale and averaged to range from 0 to 1. Cronbach's alpha was 0.66 in the Korean experiment and 0.66 in the Japanese experiment. Willingness to forgive was originally developed to assess the attitudes of the victim group. However, we believed it would be interesting to measure the Japanese people's perception of whether they should be forgiven, especially when many Japanese people believe that Japan has apologized multiple times to Korea. Figure 3.1 presents the distributions of the items in the two countries. As is evident in the figure, the Korean and Japanese people had remarkably contrasting opinions on whether the current generation should be forgiven for Japan's atrocities during the colonial period.

Attitudes about the issue of comfort women were assessed using the following four items: "Korea/Japan should listen to Japan's/Korea's arguments about historical issues, such as that of comfort women, among others," "Korea/Japan should not make any concessions on the historical issues such as comfort women," "The Korea–Japan/Japan–Korea pact on the issue of comfort women that was concluded at the end of 2015 should be kept," and "The statue of a young girl set in front of the Japanese consulate in Busan in recognition and remembrance of comfort women should be removed." The raw distributions of responses to these items are presented in Figure 3.2. These items were measured using a five-point

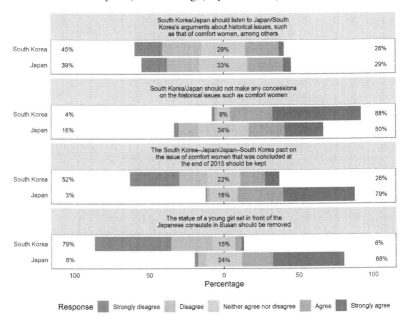

Figure 3.2 Distributions of attitudes regarding the issue of comfort women.

scale and rescaled to 0 to 1 so that higher values indicated more hard-line attitudes against the other country. As the Cronbach's alpha was lower than .60 in Korea, we analyze these items separately.

To boost the efficiency of the estimations, we included sex, age, education, ideology, and feeling thermometer scores as pretreatment covariates. Ideology was measured using an 11-point scale and rescaled to range from 0 to 1. In the analyses of the Korean experiment, feeling thermometer scores of Japan and the Japanese people were included, while those of Korea and the Korean people were used in the analyses of the Japanese experiment.

Results

We begin by analyzing the Korean experiment. First, to answer RQ1, ordinary least squares regression models were estimated with willingness to forgive and issue attitudes as outcomes (see Table A1 in the appendix). To explore the treatment effects, the coefficients of the treatments were plotted. Figure 3.3 illustrates the treatment effects on willingness to forgive. The 0 position on the horizontal axis indicates the baseline category,

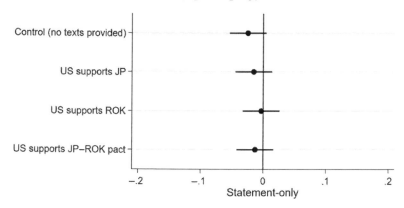

Figure 3.3 Treatment effects on willingness to forgive (Korea).

which is the statement-only group. Therefore, if a group's point estimate is located to the right of the 0 position, the group shows a higher willingness to forgive than the statement-only group. By contrast, if a group's point estimate is to the left of the 0 position, the group shows a lower willingness to forgive than the statement-only group. We use the statement-only group as the baseline because this allows us to present the effects of apology (i.e., comparing the baseline and control groups) and additional descriptions regarding the US position (i.e., comparing the baseline with the other three treatment groups) simultaneously. The bars extending to the left and right of the point estimates represent 95% confidence intervals.

Figure 3.3 shows that the control group is located to the left of the baseline (i.e., the statement-only group), meaning that reading the apologetic statement made South Koreans slightly more forgiving compared with the control group, who did not read anything. However, the difference was not statistically significant, as the 95% confidence interval covers the baseline. This result implies that mere statements of apology do not lead to forgiveness, replicating the findings on intergroup apologies. In addition, willingness to forgive did not reach the level of statistical significance among the three US position treatment groups, indicating that the perceived position of the US does not affect the level of forgiveness among the Korean people.

Next, the treatment effects on the issue attitudes are illustrated in Figure 3.4. As noted above, all the issue attitude items are coded so that the larger values mean more hard-line attitudes against the other country—in this case, Japan. Figure 3.4 indicates that most of the treatment effects are indistinguishable from the baseline. The only statistically significant effect was for the item on whether to keep the 2015 pact. The

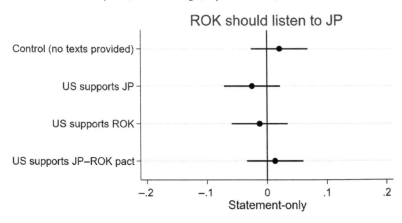

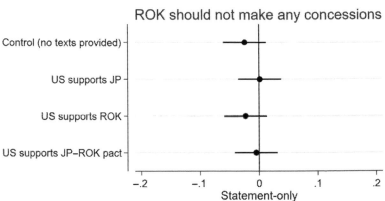

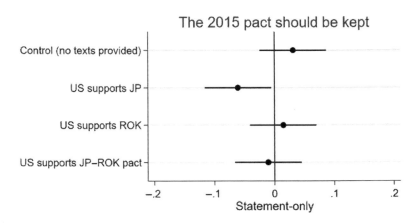

Figure 3.4 Treatment effects on issue attitudes (Korea). *(Continued)*

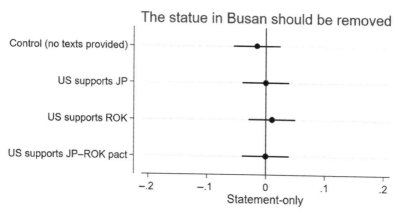

Figure 3.4 *(Continued)*

"US supports Japan" group indicated a significantly less hard-line attitude compared with the statement-only group. That is, those Koreans who read the additional description that the US stands by the Japanese government tended to think that the 2015 pact should be kept compared with those who read only about Prime Minister Abe's apologies. However, we avoid interpreting too much from this singularly significant result because of the risk of a type I error from multiple testing. The overall implication of these analyses is that the Korean people's attitudes are not amenable to the perceived position of the US.

Next, we turn to the Japanese experiment exploring RQ2. As with the Korean experiment, ordinary least squares regression models were estimated with willingness to forgive and issue attitudes as outcomes (see Table A2 in the appendix). To explore the treatment effects, the coefficients of the treatments were plotted. Figure 3.5 illustrates the treatment effects on willingness to forgive. Willingness to forgive is normally measured from the perspective of the victim group. Nevertheless, the Japanese experiment measured the extent to which Japanese people think they should be forgiven by Korean people. Therefore, it should be noted that the concept and its measurements are not equal between Korea and Japan. In Figure 3.5, the 0 position on the horizontal axis indicates the baseline category. If a group's point estimate is located to the right of the 0 position, the group agrees more strongly with the idea that the current generation of Japanese people should be forgiven by the Korean people. By contrast, if a group's point estimate is to the left to the 0 position, the group more strongly expects that the current generation of Japanese people will not be forgiven by the Korean people.

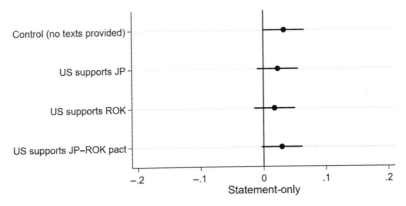

Figure 3.5 Treatment effects on willingness to forgive (Japan).

Unlike the Korean experiment, the difference between the control group and the statement-only group was significant at the 5% level. That is, when the Japanese sample read Prime Minister Abe's apologies, they tended to think they would not be forgiven by the Korean people compared with the control group, who did not read anything. The US positions did not significantly alter Japanese people's expectations about forgiveness by the South Korean people, although the "US supports Japan–Korea pact" group showed a positive effect, which was marginally significant at the 10% level.

The treatment effects on issue attitudes are illustrated in Figure 3.6. First, the difference between the control group and the statement-only group (i.e., the baseline) was significant for two of the four outcomes. Those who read Prime Minister Abe's apologies tended not to agree with ideas like Japan not needing to make any concessions and the statue in Busan being removed. That is, in line with the analysis of expected forgiveness, Japanese people who read Prime Minister Abe's statements showed less hard-line attitudes regarding the issue of comfort women. The studies on intergroup apologies have primarily examined the effects on victim groups, but these analyses indicate, at least in the context of Japan–Korea relations, that intergroup apologies have more observable effects on the perpetrator than on the victim group.

Figure 3.6 also shows some notable effects of the US position. When the US is described as supporting the position of Japan, the Japanese people tend to agree more strongly that the statue in Busan should be removed. Similar effects can be seen when the US is described as supporting the 2015 Japan–Korea pact: when the US is described as supporting

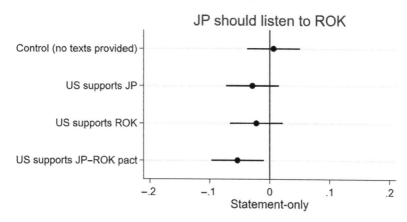

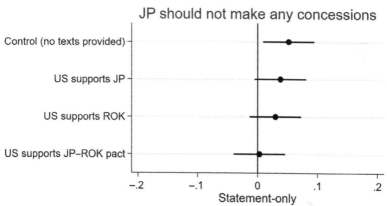

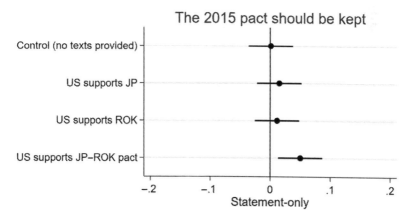

Figure 3.6 Treatment effects on issue attitudes (Japan). *(Continued)*

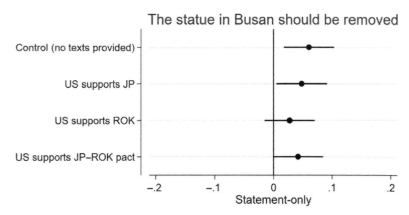

Figure 3.6 (Continued)

the 2015 pact, Japanese participants more strongly agreed with keeping the pact and removing the statue in Busan, although the latter effect was marginally significant at the 10% level. These effects indicate that when the US is perceived to be supportive of Japan's position or the 2015 pact, Japanese people tend to show more hard-line attitudes on the issue of comfort women. Japanese people may have felt that being endorsed by the US legitimized the Japanese government's official line.

However, the Japanese people also more strongly agreed that Japan should listen to Korea's arguments about historical issues when the US was described as supporting the 2015 pact. The mechanism of this effect cannot be fully unpacked with this study, but it is possible that the feeling that the US supports the pact may allow the Japanese people to listen to South Korea's arguments with a degree of leeway. In sum, when the US is perceived as supporting the 2015 pact, Japanese people tend to have more hard-line attitudes while simultaneously becoming more open to listening to Korea's arguments.

Discussion

The issue of comfort women has been a central historic disagreement between Korea and Japan. Although the governments of the two countries have tried to reconcile this issue, its remarkably divergent perceptions between the Japanese and Korean peoples have hindered a resolution. The descriptive statistics shown in Figures 3.1 and 3.2 indicate sharply conflicting views. Reconciliation between victim and perpetrator groups entails apologies. However, the extant research indicates that intergroup apologies rarely lead to forgiveness by the victim group, making it a puzzle as to why more countries have been issuing official intergroup apologies in recent years. We aimed to solve this puzzle by shedding light on the role of the third party in the process of intergroup apologies. That is, intergroup apologies can be effective depending on the position of the important third party (i.e., the US in the context of Japan–Korea relations). Moreover, previous studies have primarily examined the effects of intergroup apologies on the victim group, rendering the effects on the perpetrator group largely unexplored. By focusing on the role of a third party, and the effects on the perpetrator group, this chapter probed the conditions upon which Japan's apologies may lead to reconciliation.

Our results are consistent with previous findings: the mere occurrence of Japan's apologies did not influence a willingness to forgive or issue attitudes among Koreans. Moreover, the positions of the US were largely irrelevant to Korean attitudes, and thus failed to offer a path to reconciliation. The only exception was increased agreement with keeping the 2015 pact when the US was described as supporting Japan, though this effect was relatively small and unobserved for the other outcomes. Overall, the Korean people's unwillingness to forgive and issue attitudes are well-entrenched and thus unlikely to change from reading about Japan's past apologies and the US position.

However, we found some notable effects on Japanese people's attitudes. When the Japanese participants read about Prime Minister Abe's apologies, they became more reconciliatory and less demanding of forgiveness. Identifying these effects on the perpetrator group is a unique contribution to the literature. These findings imply that intergroup apologies can potentially lead to reconciliation not because they make the victim group more forgiving, but because they make the perpetrator group humbler and more apologetic. However, our results also indicate that the perpetrator group may become more assertive when an important third party supports their position or the agreement between the perpetrator and victim groups. The US endorsement may legitimize Japan's unwillingness to make further concessions, potentially making reconciliation more difficult. However, the US endorsement may also nudge the Japanese people to listen to Korea's arguments, which would help keep the window for dialog open.

It is also important to note some limitations of the experiments. Because of the salience of the issue, it is likely that people's attitudes are entrenched and difficult to change by a one-off treatment. Korean respondents may have known about Prime Minister Abe's apologies at the time of the experiment, although they may not have taken them as sincere. If they were familiar with the apologies, then these participants were already treated, leading to a pretreatment bias, which may have hindered the treatment effect estimations. Although this is inherent when studying a well-known issue, future studies should triangulate the methodologies to provide more conclusive evidence on the apparent ineffectiveness of intergroup apologies. It should also be noted that the age range of the participants was 20–59 years, excluding older adults. Conservative Koreans, who are arguably more sensitive to the US position, tend to be older than their liberal counterparts. Therefore, excluding those older than 59 years may have made the effects of the US position more difficult to detect in the Korean experiment.

The issue of comfort women remains a problem on the long, winding road to reconciliation between Korea and Japan. Apology is undoubtedly a key to reconciliation, yet it is not simply a matter of intergroup apologies leading directly to forgiveness. Japan has made multiple apologies, but these have not been perceived as sincere by many South Koreans for multiple reasons, including the lack of reparations from the Japanese government and revisionist gaffs by some Japanese politicians. The lack of common perception is evident in our data, as shown in Figures 3.1 and 3.2. At the same time, many Japanese people are starting to feel "apology fatigue," which would undermine their motivation to make further apologies and reconcile. The 2015 pact regarding the issue of comfort women was epoch-making because it "confirmed that the issue of comfort women was resolved finally and irreversibly." Unfortunately, however, the pact lost its effectiveness and the issue seems to be adrift, without any clear initiative toward resolution by either side.

In theory, third parties can play a crucial role in intergroup conflicts, leading to the expectation that the US can facilitate reconciliation between Japan and Korea. In fact, the 2015 pact is considered to have been pushed strongly by the US. However, our results indicate that US support for a bilateral agreement could actually harden attitudes among the Japanese, although it has also widened the window for dialog. The position of a powerful third party is thus complicated and does not necessarily facilitate reconciliation in a straightforward way. The slight glimmer of hope is the effect of apologies on the perpetrator group. Reading about apologies softens attitudes among the Japanese, which has not been previously documented in the extant literature. Reading official apologies from political leaders might remind individuals of the damage that their country inflicted on the victims, making the perpetrator group more reflexive and ready for reconciliation. The implication of these effects on the Japanese people is that the Japanese government should make its apologies to not only South Koreans, but also its own citizens.

Note

1 These values may include "expressive responding" in which the respondents engage in cheerleading for their own countries despite their true beliefs. For example, Korean people may assert that no Japanese prime ministers have apologized even when they know this happened because, for instance, the apologies were not perceived as sincere. While expressive responses cannot be ruled out, the results nevertheless show significant perceptual gaps between these countries.

References

Bennett, M., & Dewberry, C. (1994). "I've said I'm sorry, haven't I?" A study of the identity implications and constraints that apologies create for their recipients. *Current Psychology*, *13*(1), 10–20. doi:10.1007/bf02686855

Buruma, I. (1999). The joys and perils of victimhood. *The New York Review of Books*, *46*, 4–9.

Cha, V. D. (1999). *Alignment Despite Antagonism: The United States–Korea–Japan Security Triangle*. Stanford, CA: Stanford University Press.

Cha, V. D., & Kang, D. C. (2018). *Nuclear North Korea: A Debate on Engagement Strategies (updated version)*. New York, NY: Columbia University Press.

De Cremer, D., Dijk, E. V., & Pillutla, M. M. (2010). Explaining unfair offers in ultimatum games and their effects on trust: An experimental approach. *Business Ethics Quarterly*, *20*(1), 107–126. doi:10.5840/beq20102018

De Cremer, D., Pillutla, M. M., & Folmer, C. P. R. (2010). How important is an apology to you? Forecasting errors in evaluating the value of apologies. *Psychological Science*, *22*(1), 45–48. doi:10.1177/0956797610391101

Dudden, A. (2008). *Troubled Apologies among Japan, Korea, and the United States*. New York, NY: Columbia University Press.

Exline, J. J., & Baumeister, R. F. (2000). Expressing forgiveness and repentance: Benefits and barriers. In M. E. McCullough, K. I. Pargament, & C. E. Thoresen (Eds.), *Forgiveness: Theory, Research, and Practice*. New York, NY: Guilford Press. (pp. 133–155).

Exline, J. J., Baumeister, R. F., Bushman, B. J., Campbell, W. K., & Finkel, E. J. (2004). Too proud to let go: Narcissistic entitlement as a barrier to forgiveness. *Journal of Personality and Social Psychology*, *87*(6), 894–912. doi:10.1037/0022-3514.87.6.894

Harth, N. S., Hornsey, M. J., & Barlow, F. K. (2011). Emotional responses to rejection of gestures of intergroup reconciliation. *Personality and Social Psychology Bulletin*, *37*(6), 815–829. doi:10.1177/0146167211400617

Hornsey, M. J., & Wohl, M. J. A. (2013). We are sorry: Intergroup apologies and their tenuous link with intergroup forgiveness. *European Review of Social Psychology*, *24*(1), 1–31. doi:10.1080/10463283.2013.822206

Hornsey, M. J., Wohl, M. J., & Philpot, C. R. (2015). Collective apologies and their effects on forgiveness: Pessimistic evidence but constructive implications. *Australian Psychologist*, *50*(2), 106–114. doi:10.1111/ap.12087

Iokibe, K., Komiya, K., Hosoya, Y., & Miyagi, T. (2020). *History, Memory, and Politics in Postwar Japan*. Boulder, CO: Lynne Rienner.

Kim, M. (2016). *Routledge Handbook of Memory and Reconciliation in East Asia*. New York, NY: Routledge.

Kimura, K. (2019). *The Burden of the Past: Problems of Historical Perception in Japan–Korea Relations*. Ann Arbor, MI: University of Michigan Press.

Kitagawa, R., & Chu, J. A. (2021). The impact of political apologies on public opinion. *World Politics, 73*(3), 441–481. doi:10.1017/S0043887121000083

Lazare, A. (2004). *On Apology*. Oxford: Oxford University Press.

Lind, J. (2008). *Sorry States: Apologies in International Politics*. New York: Cornell University Press.

Lind, J. (2009). Apologies in international politics. *Security Studies, 18*, 517–556. doi:10.1080/09636410903132987

Mifune, N., Inamasu, K., Kohama, S., Ohtsubo, Y., & Tago, A. (2019). Social dominance orientation as an obstacle to intergroup apology. *PloS ONE, 14*(1), e0211379. https://doi.org/10.1371/journal.pone.0211379

Okimoto, T. G., Wenzel, M., & Hornsey, M. J. (2015). Apologies demanded yet devalued: Normative dilution in the age of apology. *Journal of Experimental Social Psychology, 60*, 133–136. doi:10.1016/j.jesp.2015.05.008

Philpot, C. R., & Hornsey, M. J. (2008). What happens when groups say sorry: The effect of intergroup apologies on their recipients. *Personality and Social Psychology Bulletin, 34*(4), 474–487. doi:10.1177/0146167207311283

Philpot, C. R., & Hornsey, M. J. (2011). Memory for intergroup apologies and its relationship with forgiveness. *European Journal of Social Psychology, 41*(1), 96–106. doi:10.1002/ejsp.741

Risen, J. L., & Gilovich, T. (2007). Target and observer differences in the acceptance of questionable apologies. *Journal of Personality and Social Psychology, 92*(3), 418–433. doi:10.1037/0022-3514.92.3.418

Skarlicki, D. P., Folger, R., & Gee, J. (2004). When social accounts backfire: The exacerbating effects of a polite message or an apology on reactions to an unfair outcome. *Journal of Applied Social Psychology, 34*(2), 322–341. doi:10.1111/j.1559-1816.2004.tb02550.x

Wohl, M. J. A., & Branscombe, N. R. (2005). Forgiveness and collective guilt assignment to historical perpetrator groups depend on level of social category inclusiveness. *Journal of Personality and Social Psychology, 88*(2), 288–303. doi:10.1037/0022-3514.88.2.288

Wohl, M. J. A., Hornsey, M. J., & Philpot, C. R. (2011). A critical review of official public apologies: Aims, pitfalls, and a staircase model of effectiveness. *Social Issues and Policy Review, 5*(1), 70–100. doi:10.1111/j.1751-2409.2011.01026.x

Wohl, M. J. A., Hornsey, M. J., & Bennett, S. H. (2012). Why group apologies succeed and fail: Intergroup forgiveness and the role of primary and secondary emotions. *Journal of Personality and Social Psychology, 102*(2), 306–322. doi:10.1037/a0024838

Wohl, M. J. A., Matheson, K., Branscombe, N. R., & Anisman, H. (2013). Victim and perpetrator groups responses to the Canadian government's apology for the head tax on Chinese immigrants and the moderating influence of collective guilt. *Political Psychology, 34*(5), 713–729. doi:10.1111/pops.12017

4 Analyzing "anti-Korean" hate books in Japan[1]

Hongchun Lee

Why are many "Kenkanbon" (anti-Korean hate books) published in Japan to express contempt for a particular country and plant discriminatory feelings against a particular people? Oizumi et al. (2015) defines "heitobon" (hate books) as "books that mock other nations and incite ethnic discrimination and chauvinism." When "other nations" is replaced with "South Korea," such books still constitute Kenkanbon. Why has that trend persisted? Why do many bookstores continue to sell Kenkanbon? Why do so many publishers produce such material? Why do many authors incite chauvinism by ridiculing a specific ethnic group and their country? We naturally ask these questions when we see many Kenkanbon piled up in large bookstores in Japan. These "Kenkan–Kenchubon" (anti-Korean and anti-Chinese books) are an established book genre in Japan (Asahi Shimbun, 2017). However, criticism within the publishing industry is rare.

Kenkanbon reflects the revisionist historical views of Japanese conservatives, and specifically targets South Korea (hereafter, Korea) and its people (Jimbo, 2020). Kenkanbon are also known to have a strong association with discriminatory behavior, such as hate speech. This has become a salient issue in relation to Korean minorities in Japan, and the United Nations Commission on Eliminating Racial Discrimination has recommended that the Japanese government impose legal regulation. At anti-Korean rallies, strong hate speech may be heard, such as "Good or bad, kill all the Koreans!" and "Koreans, hang yourselves! Drink poison! Leap to your death!" Echoing the intense negativity of hate speech, an avalanche of derogatory words, sophistry, falsification, lies, and conspiracy theories can be found in Kenkanbon (Han, 2010).

Kenkanbon first appeared in 1993, but in 2005 they began to attract wider attention in Japanese society, and since 2012, such publications have boomed. Despite the shrinking publishing market in Japan, the Kenkanbon boom has persisted and produced a significant number of anti-Korean hate books. Publishers are responsible for creating this surge (Kato, Akedo, &

DOI: 10.4324/9781003143536-4

Kambara, 2014) and some attempts have been made to probe the driving factors (Oizumi et al., 2015). Another line of criticism focused on the unique Japanese distribution system for books, which allegedly helped the flourishing Kenkanbon market (Nagae, 2019).

However, several more detailed questions have been rarely investigated. What kinds of Kenkanbon are published? Who are the authors? Who are the publishers? How diverse are the authors and publishers, and how have they changed? How are the Kenkanbon trends related to changes in Japan–Korea relations? Rather than mere summaries of chauvinism on a macroeconomic basis, such as the publishing slump, microlevel examinations are necessary to derive a better understanding of the underlying mechanisms of the Kenkanbon boom.

What does "Kenkan" (hating Korea) mean?

Before discussing when it began, the concept of "Kenkan" (hating Korea) needs to be elaborated. Digital Kojien, a major Japanese encyclopedia, briefly defines Kenkan as "having a sense of adversity toward Korea and Koreans."[2] Digital Kojien also introduces "the emotion of disliking Koreans" as an example of Kenkan. Therefore, Kenkanbon do not criticize South Korean (hereafter, Korean) foreign policy based on rational arguments, but are intended to incite negative sentiment against South Korea and its people (Ishibashi, 2020). Kenkanbon work in tandem with hate speech rallies that excoriate, ridicule, denigrate, and pour contempt on South Koreans.[3] Specifically, Kenkanbon demand the expulsion of Korean ethnic minorities from Japan and sometimes call for physical harm, such as genocide.[4]

The term "Kenkan" first appeared in the media in an *Asahi Shimbun* editorial on August 12, 1992.[5] At that time, only the mass media used this term, and the public did not recognize it as a social reality until 2012, when Kenkan was manifested in hate speech rallies. According to a survey conducted by the Ministry of Justice, 1,152 hate speech demonstrations were held between 2012 and 2015, and most targeted Koreans[6] (Ministry of Justice, 2016). These rallies have been attributed to the deteriorating bilateral relations between Japan and Korea; several incidents during this period were related to a territorial dispute over Dokdo/Takeshima Island, and issues arose over "comfort women" during World War II, restrictions on the importation of Japanese marine products after the 2011 Fukushima Daiichi nuclear accident, the name of the Sea of Japan/East Sea, and a stolen Buddha statue. As a result, the number of people who felt an affinity toward Korea decreased sharply from 40.7% in 2012 to 31.5% in 2014, which was a record low since the survey started in 1978

(Cabinet Office, 2014).[7] Hate speech is concentrated in four prefectures in the Kanto region, mainly in Tokyo, followed by major cities such as Osaka, Kyoto, and Hyogo Prefectures.[8] The anti-hate speech poster created by the Japanese Ministry of Justice called for an end to "discriminatory words and actions that aim to exclude people of a particular ethnicity or nationality."[9]

Hate speech rallies are regarded as discriminatory because their slogans call for the elimination of specific nations, ethnicities, and races associated with anti-immigration, prejudice, and chauvinistic nationalism (Tanabe, 2015). In Japan, the discriminatory exclusivism that advocates for the exclusion of foreign people, ideas, and products is associated with patriotism and nationalism based on the myth of Japanese mono-ethnicity. Patriotism is a strong driver of anti-Chinese and anti-Korean sentiments in Japan. Typical examples are the activities of the Zaitokukai, an organization known for its radical exclusionary actions against Korean residents in Japan.[10] What is unique about Japanese chauvinism is that it targets advanced nations such as Korea rather than vulnerable developing nations. Korea was a Japanese colony in the past, but its recent cultural and historical development has never been slower than that of Japan.

The concept of Kenkan is related to xenophobia (Higuchi, 2014). According to Lee (2017, 2018, 2019), xenophobia has the following subconcepts: (a) negative attitudes toward foreign nationals, who are regarded as political outgroup members; (b) racism against ethnic minorities; (c) perceptions of a political threat; and (d) perception of a cultural threat. Xenophobia in Japan is promoted by political pride (Tanabe, 2015, 2018), which, in turn, strongly influences patriotism (Higuchi, 2014). It can be said that Kenkan is a form of xenophobia mainly directed at Koreans and South Korea.

What is Kenkanbon?

In November 2005, the *New York Times* reported booming sales of Kenkanbon in Japan. In the article, the terms "Kenkanryu" (hating the "Korean wave") and "Kenkan ishiki" (anti-Korean sentiments) were introduced. The article also introduced the anti-Korean assertions of Kenkanbon, such as that "it is not an exaggeration to say that Japan built South Korea today" and attributed these assertions to differences between Japan and Korean understandings of the colonial period of history (Onishi, 2005).

Although the *New York Times* article made the world aware of the Kenkanbon, it did not clarify that this phenomenon is unique to Japan and not observed in Korea. That is, although anti-Japanese sentiment is not unusual in Korea, such books are rare. Even a search of the database of *Sankei Shimbun*, a conservative newspaper critical of Korea, did not find any "hate books" about Japan. If such a book were published, *Sankei Shimbun* and conservative newspapers critical of Korea would certainly have reported it. Therefore, it is reasonable to assume that there are no anti-Japan/anti-Japanese equivalents of Kenkanbon.[11] In summary, although the bitter sentiments between Japan and Korea are by and large mutual, the hate book publication boom is unique to Japan.

Acceptance of Kenkanbon by Japanese bookstores

How did Japanese bookstores start to sell Kenkanbon? The boom started with a magazine book called *Manga Kenkanryu* (anti-Korean wave comics) published in 2005. It was reported that over a million copies were issued (Uozumi, 2020). Kenkanbon such as *Minikui Kankoku-jin: Wareware wa nitteishihai wo sakebi sugiru* (Ugly South Korean people: We cry over Japanese imperial rule too much) (Park, 1993) had been published previously. However, it was *Manga Kenkanryu* that popularized Kenkanbon and established the genre. In the 2010s, the publication of Kenkanbon shifted from magazines to pocket-sized paperbacks ("shinsyo" in Japanese), and the broader genre of "Kenkan/Kenchubon" (anti-Korea/anti-China books) was established.

The Kenkanbon publishing boom has generally been explained in three ways. The first explanation attributes the boom to the increasing chauvinism of Japanese society. The rise of the "netto uyoku" (the online right-wing movement), the birth of Zaitokukai, and the frequent hate speech rallies have been deemed to be antecedents of the flourishing Kenkanbon. The second explanation focuses on the plight of the publishing industry. The publishing industry's sales peaked in 1996; since then, sales have declined steadily. By 2013, the market had halved in size compared with the peak. During the slump, one genre that could mitigate the publishers' plight was Kenkanbon. When *Manga Kenkaryu* became a best seller in 2005, more than a few publishers started to publish books with the same theme (Nam, 2020). The third explanation focuses on the unique distribution system of books in Japan. Although this is related to the second explanation in that they both blame bookstores' commercialism, the unique distribution system, called "Mihakarai Haihon" (proactive book delivery system), warrants special attention (Nagae, 2019).

Mihakarai Haihon is a process of selecting and distributing books at the discretion of the book agencies that mediate between publishers and bookstores. Book agencies consider the bookstores' size, location, and customer base to decide which books are delivered and sold. For example, book agencies select business books for sale in office districts, technology books in districts with many students, and so on (Nishimura, 2020). Therefore, the agencies can force bookstores to sell the selected books even when they are not ordered. By this process, book agencies are known to distribute Kenkanbon preferentially to bookstores with high sales volume. This is one cause of the Kenkanbon boom (Nishimura, 2020).

Another system related to the Kenkanbon boom is "Itaku Hanbai" (the consignment sales system), whereby books are purchased with return conditions. Bookstores can return unsold books to publishers, but payment is made in advance on delivery by book agencies (Ishioka, 2001). This system has created a structure in which sensationalist books, such as Kenkanbon, are mass-produced to secure short-term profits for publishers. In reality, the initial demand for discriminatory books such as Kenkanbon was not great. However, because bookstores pay for books when they are distributed, they have no choice but to put them on the shelves even if they are not expected to sell well. In this way, even with little demand, Kenkanbon began to have a significant presence in bookstores, sparking the boom (Ishioka, 2001).

Analysis of Kenkanbon

Authors

Understanding the authors of Kenkanbon is essential. By identifying the authors and their attributes, we can understand the background of the phenomenon. I first analyze the authors of 304 Kenkanbon published from 1993 to 2020. In this study, we listed Kenkanbon based on the following three criteria. First, I listed all the books exhibited at the Kenkan Publications Exhibition held in 2014 at the Korean National Assembly. Next, I added the titles identified as Kenkanbon by Oizumi et al. (2015) and Japanese magazines (Daily SPA!, 2017; Shindo, 2018; Toyo Keizai, 2015). Finally, from the listed books, I manually selected those that incite discriminatory sentiment toward Korea or Korean people. Figure 4.1 shows the numbers of Kenkanbon and authors in each fiscal year. The total number of authors was 411. The trends of Kenkanbon and their authors are similar, but it is noteworthy that in 2006 and 2014, some Kenkanbon were written by multiple authors. This is arguably due to the difficulty of finding new authors to meet the increasing demand.[12] In other words, Kenkanbon tend to be published repeatedly by a limited number of authors.

Who are the authors of Kenkanbon? Their names are listed in Table 4.1. Table 4.1 shows that O Sonfa writes the most; she has written 30 Kenkanbon, including coauthored books. She is a Korean born in Jeju Island who came to Japan in 1983. She completed her master's program

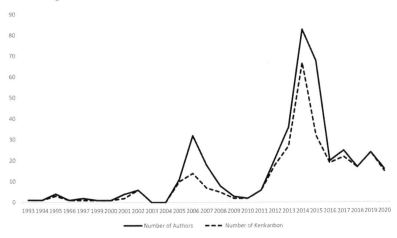

Figure 4.1 Trends in the numbers of Kenkanbon and authors.

at the Tokyo University of Foreign Studies and is currently a professor at Takushoku University in Japan. She acquired Japanese nationality in 1998. In 1990, she drew attention by publishing *Shin Sukato no Kaze* (*The New Wind to Skirt*) (O, 2000). Although she now holds Japanese nationality, she claims that the Kenkanbon she wrote criticizes Korea from the Korean perspective. The second most productive author is Ko Bunyu of Taiwanese origin, who was involved in 28 Kenkanbon. He came to Japan in 1964. After graduating from Waseda University, he obtained a master's degree from Meiji University. The third place was held by Sincerelee and Katsumi Murotani, both of whom wrote 18 Kenkanbon. Sincerelee was born in Korea in 1970. He closed his dental clinic and moved to Japan in 2017 and opened a blog that was critical of Korea, which has become very popular,

Table 4.1 Authors of Kenkanbon

Name	Number of publications	Number of publishers	Name	Number of publications	Number of publishers
O, Sonfa	30	12	Yamano, Sharin	9	2
Ko, Bunyu	28	14	Genkotsu, Takufumi	8	3
Sincerelee	18	2	Sakurai, Makoto	8	3
Murotani, Katsumi	18	9	Mitsubashi, Takaaki	7	2
Seki, Hei	11	7	Toyota, Aritsune	7	2

with about 100,000 daily page views. The fifth most prolific author is Seki Hei, who has written 11 Kenkanbon. Born in Sichuan Province, China, in 1962, he graduated from Peking University. After completing his doctoral program at Kobe University in 1995, he began writing his critiques. He acquired Japanese nationality in 2007.

These analyses yield two findings. The authors of Kenkanbon are a small group of people who publish many works. The top 10 authors appear 144 times and account for 35% of the Kenkanbon. In other words, 2.4% of the authors were involved in 35% of the published Kenkanbon. This indicates that the Kenkanbon boom may have been staged by a few authors and do not necessarily reflect the views of many authors. The second finding is that the nationalities of the authors are rather diverse; in many cases, they are of non-Japanese origin. Among the top five authors, four were born abroad and later obtained Japanese nationality. Two are of South Korean origin, one is from China and the other is from Taiwan. The fact that Kenkanbon are written not only by Japanese authors but also by authors from Korea and other countries may have the effect of boosting the perceived objectivity and validity of their views.

Publishers

Table 4.2 shows the Kenkanbon that have ranked among the monthly top 20 best sellers since 2013. These data were obtained from the AJPEA

Table 4.2 Kenkanbon that ranked in the top 20 monthly sales

Year	Title	Name	Publisher
2013	Bokanron	Murotani, Katsumi	Sankei Shimbun
2014	Bokanron	Murotani, Katsumi	Sankei Shimbun
	South Korean stories so bad that they're funny	Takeda, Tsuneyasu	Business Sha
	Shameful South Korea theory by Koreans	Sincerelee	Fusosha
2017	The tragedy of Chinese and South Koreans ruled by Confucianism	Gilbert, Kent	Kodansha
2019	South Korea: the price of lies	Takahashi, Yoichi	Fusosha
	Disease called South Korea	Monthly Hanada	Asuka Shinsha

Source: Publishing Sciences Laboratory; author's summary of monthly best sellers

(All Japan Magazine and Book Publishers and Editors Association).[13] In 2013, *Bokanron* (Appalling Korea), published by Sankei Shimbun, sold nearly 300,000 copies and ranked in the top 20. Later, this book became the 2014 annual best seller in the nonfiction paperback category. In 2014, *Kankokujin ni yoru chikanron* (Shameful Korea theory by Koreans) published by Fusosha and *Waraeru hodo tachi ga warui Kannkoku no hanashi* (Korean stories so bad that they're funny) published by Business Sha ranked in the top 20. The former sold more than 200,000 copies, and its author, Sincerelee, has published 16 books through Fusosha, accounting for about a half of Fusosha's Kenkanbon.[14] In 2017, Kent Gilbert, an American lawyer, published *Jyukyo ni shihai sareta Chugokujin to Kankokujin* (The tragedy of Chinese and Koreans ruled by Confucianism), which sold about 500,000 copies.[15] These data indicate the strong sales of Kenkanbon in the recent Japanese book market. Next, I examine the publishers of Kenkanbon in detail.

Table 4.3 shows the 10 publishers with the largest number of Kenkanbon publications. Fusosha has published 36 books and is the most active publisher of Kenkanbon. Fusosha is known for its criticism of traditional history textbooks for indoctrinating readers with the so-called self-tormenting historical view. It has also published the *New History Textbook*, produced under the supervision of the Society for the Creation of New History Textbooks, which is known for its revisionist views of modern history. Next, Wac and Takarajimasha have published 20 Kenkanbon each. Shinyusha, which published *Manga Kenkanryu* and ignited the Kenkanbon publishing boom, has released 16 books and ranks seventh. In total, 178 Kenkanbon have been released by the top 10 publishers, accounting for 58% of all Kenkanbon published between 1993 and 2020. That is, there are several specific publishers of Kenkanbon. This concentration of publishers shows that recession alone cannot explain the Kenkanbon boom.

Table 4.3 Number of Kenkanbon by publisher

Rank	Publisher	# of Kenkanbon	Rank	Publisher	# of Kenkanbon
1	Fusosha	36	6	Shodensha	16
2	Wac	20	7	Shinyusha	16
	Takarajimasha	20	8	Shogakukan	14
4	Tokuma Shoten	19	9	Seirindo	12
5	PHP Kenkyusho	17	10	Business Sha	8

Period: 1993–2020.

If the publishing recession were the cause, many other smaller publishers would also have published Kenkanbon.

Plight of publishers

Sales of publications in 2020 totaled 1.2 trillion yen, which is about half of the 2.3 trillion yen in 2000 (Table 4.4). In 2005, when Kenkanbon first became best sellers, sales had fallen by 2.1% from the previous fiscal year. In 2014, sales of Japanese books and magazines were 1.6 trillion yen, a decline of 80 billion yen from the previous year, which was the most significant drop since 1997.[16] Sales of publications in 2015, when the largest number of Kenkanbon were published, declined by 5.3% from the previous year. These numbers indicate that many Kenkanbon were published in reaction to the shrinking book market. In fact, there is a negative correlation ($r = -0.58$) between the number of published Kenkanbon and annual book sales. The more the publishing industry suffers, the more Kenkanbon tend to be published.

Table 4.4 Declining sales in the publishing industry

Year	(100 million yen)		
	Books	*Magazines*	*Total*
2000	9,706	14,261	23,966
2001	9,456	13,794	23,250
2002	9,490	13,616	23,105
2003	9,056	13,222	22,278
2004	9,429	12,998	22,428
2005	9,197	12,767	21,964
2006	9,326	12,200	21,525
2007	9,026	11,827	20,853
2008	8,878	11,299	20,177
2009	8,492	10,864	19,356
2010	8,213	10,535	18,748
2011	8,198	9,844	18,042
2012	8,013	9,385	17,398
2013	7,851	8,972	16,823
2014	7,544	8,520	16,065
2015	7,419	7,801	15,220
2016	7,370	7,339	14,709
2017	7,152	6,548	13,701
2018	6,991	5,930	12,921
2019	6,723	5,637	12,360
2020	6,661	5,576	12,237

Source: A monthly report of publications, January 2021 issue.

This indicates that publishers in recession are increasingly dependent on sales of Kenkanbon.

Themes of Kenkanbon

Kenkanbon titles typically sensationally summarize the content to attract the attention of potential readers. To probe deeper into their content, I conducted a text analysis of their titles, and the results are shown in Table 4.5. Naturally, the most frequent words in the titles are "South Korea." The name appeared 288 times in 311 titles (96% of 311 Kenkanbon), showing that Kenkanbon clearly targeted Korea.

Other than "South Korea," Kenkanbon titles frequently include the names of geographical locations and countries. For example, "Japan" appears 95 times, "China" 47 times, "South Korea" 15 times, and "North Korea" 10 times. Titles with the word "Japan" use the words in contexts such as "Japan beats South Korea," "South Korea yearns for Japan," "South Korea interrupts while holding Japan's ankle," and "Korea has been modernized by Japanese colonization." The term "anti-Japanese" is used in titles such as *Why does South Korea have an anti-Japanese national policy?* These titles give the impression that the anti-Japanese movement is a governmental policy in Korea. The term "anti-Japanese" is also used to convey groundless assertions, as can be seen in the title *The self-destruction of anti-Japanese South Korea has begun.* The term "economy" refers to the wishful prediction of misfortune and collapse of the Korean economy. "Comfort women" are a lingering issue between Japan and Korea, but in Kenkanbon titles, the term implies that comfort women were prostitutes

Table 4.5 Frequently used words in Kenkanbon titles

Word	Part of speech	Freq.	Word	Part of speech	Freq.
South Korea	Noun	288	Lie	Noun	11
anti-Japanese	Noun	102	identity	Noun	10
Japan	Noun	95	North Korea	Noun	10
dislike	Noun	50	problem	Noun	9
China	Noun	47	in the world	Noun	8
history	Noun	28	Know	Verb	7
truth	Noun	27	comfort women	Noun	7
Korea	Noun	15	look at	Verb	6
economy	Noun	14	fabrication	Noun	6
Comics	Noun	12			

Minimum frequency of words was six occurrences.

"Japan" is the sum of the frequencies of the words "Japanese" and "Japan," while "China" is the sum of the frequencies of "Chinese" and "China."

and that the UN and Korea wrongly propagated the claim that comfort women were sex slaves.

Association with public opinion

It took more than 10 years for the first Kenkanbon boom to hit following the first publication in 1993; however, it did not continue because the relationship between the two countries was relatively good. Japan and South Korea co-hosted the FIFA World Cup in 2002 and at the same time, the "Korean wave" (Hallyu) hit Japan. The relatively good relationship prevented the Kenkanbon boom from continuing. However, the Kenkanbon boom came back in 2011 on a larger scale when the bilateral Japan–Korea relations rapidly deteriorated owing to a series of events, including the former President Lee Myung-bak's landing on Dokdo/Takeshima in 2012 and his demand for an apology from the Japanese Emperor. Publishers with sluggish sales did not miss this opportunity (Jo 2016, Hirano, 2017). Were Kenkanbon sales correlated with the ebb and flow of Japan–Korea relations? More specifically, is the negative public opinion of Korea related to the publication of Kenkanbon? If an increasing number of Japanese people harbor negative views of Korea, Kenkanbon should provide a business opportunity for publishers. I consider this question by examining trends in Japanese public opinion and Kenkanbon publishing.

According to the *Public Opinion Survey on Diplomacy* conducted by the Cabinet Office of Japan, the affinity felt toward Korea sharply declined in 2011. In 2019, those who did not feel an affinity with Korea reached 71.5%, which was a record high since 1978, when the survey started. Before 2011, there was a rise of negativity in 2005 and 2006, which coincided with the publication of best seller *Manga Kenkanryu*. After that, until 2011, publication of Kenkanbon and negativity toward Korea both declined.[17]

Figure 4.2 juxtaposes the publication trends of Kenkanbon and the proportion of people who do not feel an affinity with Korea. The publication trend indicates that the period can roughly be divided into two parts: from 1993 to 2011, when Kenkanbon publication began, and from 2012 to 2019, when the second and larger Kenkanbon boom was observed. In the earlier period, the Japan–Korea relationship generally improved: the proportion of people who do not feel an affinity was generally lower than before 2. The latter period from 2012 to 2019 matches the rapidly declining sense of affinity among the Japanese public. In fact, 73% of the Kenkanbon analyzed in this chapter were published during this second period. The simple correlation between the two trends indicates a significant association ($r = 0.61$).

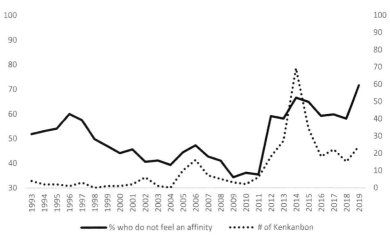

Figure 4.2 Negativity toward Korea and publications of Kenkanbon.

Who buys Kenkanbon?

It is reported that Kenkanbon readers are primarily men in their 30s to
50s (Toyo Keizai, 2015), and this age group overlaps with the readership
of pocket-sized paperbacks ("shinsyo"). For example, of those who purchased *Bokanron*, a pocket-sized paperback Kenkanbon published in 2013,
35.0% were men in their 30s and 40s, and 39.8% were men in their 50s
or over (Toyo Keizai, 2015). Of those who purchased *Kankokujin ni yoru
chikanron* written by Sincerelee in 2014, 29.3% were men in their 30s and
40s and 36.7% were men in their 50s or over (Toyo Keizai, 2015). These
numbers are in line with the fact that anti-Korean sentiment is stronger
in the middle-aged to older generations (Cabinet Office, Government of
Japan, n.d.).

I do not argue that the buyers of Kenkanbon are mostly chauvinistic
right-wing extremists. Right-wing extremists may see Kenkanbon featured
in bookstores or learn about them on social media, but in this respect, they
are little different from ordinary readers. According to a survey by Furuya
(2013), right-wing people who are active on the Internet are mostly under
40 years old, which does not match the demographics of mainstream buyers of Kenkanbon.

Will there be another Kenkanbon boom? As mentioned above, the
main buyers are middle-aged and older males, and Kenkanbon do not
sell well among younger generations. Considering these characteristics of
the Kenkanbon market, it is unlikely that the boom will spread to other
generations. As shown in Figure 4.1, Kenkanbon publication peaked in

2014 and has been on a downward trend. In recent years, the publishing industry seems to be more interested in publishing patriotic "great Japan books," with hyperbolic boasts about Japan's global reputation, rather than Kenkanbon. For example, Tsuneyasu Takeda, who once wrote a Kenkanbon, published a book in 2010 titled *Why is Japan the World's Most Popular Country?*, which had sold more than 500,000 copies by the end of 2014 (Toyo Keizai, 2015).

Conclusion

Kenkanbon are an unusual phenomenon whereby hate communication is openly published to arouse contempt, prejudice, and discrimination toward the neighboring country of South Korea and its people. Kenkanbon are not intended to criticize the Korean government but explicitly to incite discriminatory sentiments. In this sense, Kenkanbon focus on emotional agitation rather than logical explanations or persuasion.

What kinds of authors and publishers are involved in such publications? What themes are salient? How are trends in Kenkanbon linked to the ebbs and flow of Japan–Korea relations? To answer these questions, I conducted a content analysis of Kenkanbon published between 1993 and 2019. Specifically, I analyzed their authors, publishers, and the themes. In addition, I probed the potential causes of the rise of Kenkanbon by analyzing the plight of the publication industry, the unique book distribution system, and the linkage between the Kenkanbon boom and Japan–Korea relations. The results of the analyses are summarized below.

The authorship of Kenkanbon is concentrated on a few highly productive authors: the top 10 authors with the most publications wrote 35% of the books analyzed. In addition, in 2014 and 2015, when the Kenkanbon boom peaked, the supply of authors could not keep up and many books were written by multiple coauthors. In addition, many of the authors of Kenkanbon were born in other countries then came to Japan and became naturalized citizens. The above results show that few people lead the Kenkan discussions, and the Kenkanbon publishing boom did not initially represent Japanese public opinion. The analysis also indicates that titles concerning conflicts between Japan and Korea, such as comfort women and Dokdo/Takeshima, are infrequent. Rather, titles expressing a desire for the collapse of the Korean economy or baseless accusations that Korea is engaged in various fabrications were more frequent. This result suggests that Kenkanbon are not related to policy discussions on contentious issues in Japan–Korea relations, but are primarily driven by sensationalism to incite unfounded prejudice and discrimination.

The analysis revealed that the top 10 publishers were responsible for 177 Kenkanbon, accounting for 58% of the total. One motivation to publish such material is the shrinking book market. As book sales continue to decline, publishers are forced to sell whatever books they can. In fact, there is a correlation between the decline in the size of the book market and the Kenkanbon boom. Therefore, a likely primary cause of the boom is the structural recession in publishing. In addition to the plight of the publishing industry, it is also likely that common practices, such as Mihakarai Haihon and Itaku Hanbai, have increased the presence of Kenkanbon. Because of these practices, book agencies—the intermediaries between publishers and bookstores—select and distribute books for display in bookstores, regardless of whether they sell well or not. This made Kenkanbon visible in bookstores and laid the foundation for the boom.

In conclusion, it is difficult to explain the Kenkanbon boom solely in terms of the increasing chauvinism of the Japanese public. Although deteriorating sentiment toward Korea seems to be associated with Kenkanbon sales, there are likely to be multiple causes of the boom, such as the shrinking publishing market and the unique business practices of the book industry. These multiple factors interacted to create the Kenkanbon boom. Although I argue that the boom is unlikely to reemerge in the foreseeable future, it is necessary to pay close attention to the changing Japanese society to prevent discriminatory Kenkanbon from causing undue damage to Japan–Korea relations.

Notes

1 This work was supported by JSPS KAKENHI Grant Number 18K11998.
2 Digital Kojien, accessed on February 4, 2021
3 The themes of the hate speech demonstrations include the comfort women, the Dokdo/Takeshima dispute, the indictment of the *Sankei Shimbun* Seoul bureau chief, abductions by North Korea, North Korean nuclear weapons, and the Senkaku Islands.
4 *Report on the Fact-finding Survey on Hate Speech* by the Ministry of Justice (2016)
5 Asahi Shimbun, August 12, 1992, "I am concerned about mutual dislike between Japan and the ROK."
6 http://www.moj.go.jp/JINKEN/stophatespeech_chousa.html
7 Cabinet Office, Public *Opinion Survey on Diplomacy*, October 2014
8 Legal Minister, 2016, *Fact-finding Survey on Hate Speech*
9 http://www.moj.go.jp/content/001303355.pdf
10 Zainichi Tokken o Yurusanai Shinmin no Kai (Association of Citizens against the Special Privileges of Korean Residents in Japan)
11 Search keywords were "hate" and "publish." The search period was from 1992 to the present. A search of the *Asahi Shimbun* database also yielded no results.

12 If a book has more than one editor/author, each name is counted individually.
13 Details are here. https://www.ajpea.or.jp/bestseller/index.html
14 Tohan survey.
15 https://mainichi.jp/articles/20180131/dde/012/040/003000c
16 Toyo Keizai (2015), Vol. 6570, p.84.
17 Public Opinion Poll on Foreign Affairs: https://survey.gov-online.go.jp/r01/r01-gaiko/2-1.html

References

Asahi Shimbun (1992). *Concerned about mutual "hatred" between Japan and South Korea*. August 12. (In Japanese)

Asahi Shimbun (2017). *Analysis of hundreds of thousands of comments on the Internet shows that "hate Korea" and "hate China" are widespread*. April 28. https://www.asahi.com/articles/DA3S12913504.html (In Japanese)

Cabinet Office, Government of Japan. (n.d.). Public Opinion on Diplomacy. https://survey.gov-online.go.jp/index-gai.html

Daily SPA! (2017). *Why do "hate books" keep selling?* Retrieved April 20, 2021, from https://nikkan-spa.jp/spa_feature_group_name/%E3%81%AA%E3%81%9C%EF%BC%BB%E3%83%98%E3%82%A4%E3%83%88%E6%9C%AC%EF%BC%BD%E3%81%AF%E5%A3%B2%E3%82%8C%E7%B6%9A%E3%81%91%E3%82%8B%E3%81%AE%E3%81%8B%EF%BC%9F

Furuya, T. (2013). *Netto uyokuno gyakushu* (Cyber right-wingers' counterattack). Tokyo: Souwasha.

Han, Y. (2010). Anti-Korean and anti-Japanese: from Kenkanryu (hate Korean). *The Waseda Journal of Social Sciences*, 16, 132–147. (In Japanese)

Higuchi, N. (2014). *Japanese style xenophobia: Zaitokukai, suffrage for foreign nationals, and East Asian geopolitics*. Nagoya: Nagoya University Press. (In Japanese)

Hirano, M. (2017). Resonance between mass media and social media in Japan–South Korea relations: Changing public sentiment through media coverage. *Nara Prefectural University Research Report*, 9, 125–142. (In Japanese)

Ishibashi, T. (2020). The journalist who founded 'Hate Japan' in Korea realizes the mistake. *President Online*. https://president.jp/articles/-/32893 (In Japanese)

Ishioka, K. (2001). *Copyright law and antitrust law*. Tokyo: Keio University Press. (In Japanese)

Jimbo, Y. (2020). Why are 'hate books against China and Korea' placed in bookstores? Thinking about the complex and intertwined industry structure surrounding publishers, distributors, and bookstores. Retrieved February 17, 2020, from https://finders.me/articles.php?id=1675 (In Japanese)

Jo, G. J. (2016). Anti-Korean sentiment as an echo of anti-Japanese sentiment. *Journal of Asiatic Studies*, 59(1), 250–281. (In Korean)

Kato, N., Akedo, T., & Kambara, H. (2014). *No hate! Considering the producer responsibility for publishing*. Tokyo: Korokara. (In Japanese)

Lee, H. (2017). Publishing media and xenophobia: An analysis of Kenkanbon. *Journal of Information Studies*, 18, 109–118. (In Japanese)

Lee, H. (2018). A survey on the attitudes of people who come into contact with "hate-Korea" information. *Journal of Information Studies, 19*, 117–124. (In Japanese)

Lee, H. (2019). An analysis of the sources of dislike for Korea. *Journal of Information Studies, 20*, 92–99. (In Japanese)

Nagae, A. (2019). I used to love bookstores: Behind the scenes of making and selling overflowing hate books. Tokyo: Tarojiro-sha Editus. (In Japanese)

Nam, B. (2020). Retrogression and proliferation in literary thought. *Honyaku no Bunka/Bunka no Honyaku, 15*, 71–85. doi/10.14945/00027400 (In Japanese)

Nishimura, M. (2020). Necessary changes in the publishing distribution structure and systems in Japan. *The Papers and Proceedings of Economics, 159*, 131–153. http://hdl.handle.net/10723/00003801 (In Japanese)

Oh, Sonfa (2000). *The new wind to skirt.* Tokyo: Kadokawa. (In Japanese)

Oizumi, M., Kimura, M., Kato, N., & Kajita, Y. (2015). *Farewell, hate books! Behind the boom in anti-Korean and anti-Chinese books.* Tokyo: Korokara. (In Japanese)

Onishi, N. (2005). Ugly images of Asian rivals become best sellers in Japan. Retrieved April 20, 2021, from https://www.nytimes.com/2005/11/19/world/asia/ugly-images-of-asian-rivals-become-best-sellers-in-japan.html

Shindo, K. (2018). Inconvenient truths (books) are eliminated by faceless blackmailers. *WiLL, 159*, 246–251. (In Japanese)

Tanabe, S. (2015). Reflections on the Symposium "Sociological approaches to chauvinism." *Sociological Theory and Methods, 30*(2), 319–328. https://doi.org/10.11218/ojjams.30.319 (In Japanese)

Tanabe, S. (2018). A statistical investigation of anti-Korean sentiments in Japan: Comparative analysis of 2009 and 2013 data. *Bulletin of the Graduate Division of Letters, Arts and Sciences of Waseda University, 63*, 67–82. (In Japanese)

Toyo Keizai (2015). *The background of the "Japan is Amazing" business model: Who are the readers of patriotic books?* January 17. (In Japanese)

Uozumi, A. (2020). *Is the "publishing business" the priority? Kodansha's "current position" being questioned.* https://gendai.ismedia.jp/articles/-/70320?imp=0 (In Japanese)

5 Network analysis of the tweets on South Korea–Japan conflict

A case of the trade dispute in 2019

Dongwoo Lim, Fujio Toriumi, Kaori Hayashi

Before opening this book, what media were you using to receive local and world news? They could be newspapers, TV news shows, or portal sites. In many countries, news is now distributed through social media. According to Reuters' Digital News Report 2020, 48% of people in the US, 44% in South Korea (hereafter, Korea), and 25% in Japan cited social media as their source of news (Newman et al., 2020).

Unlike TV and newspapers, social media allow people to consume news in an "active and intentional" way. A typical example is Twitter's "retweeting." Kim (2013) studied reasons for retweeting on Twitter, finding the remarkable reason that retweeting brought self-satisfaction through empathy and sharing. He also noted that for this purpose, there is a tendency mainly to retweet topical and informative content. In other words, retweets can be interpreted as an act of actively disseminating others' tweets to share information with other users and receive feedback. Another example of active news consumption is "link posting." If you are a Twitter user, you have probably quoted hyperlinks from news you read on portal sites or other media in your Twitter messages. This is especially important in the media environments of Japan and Korea because the proportion of news accessed through portal sites is overwhelmingly high in these two countries. The aforementioned Digital News Report 2020 surveyed rankings of online site usage, including both portal and media sites, with Yahoo News (58%) ranking first in Japan, and Naver (62%) and Daum (32%) ranking in first and second positions in Korea. It can be seen that far more people are exposed to news through portals than those who directly access media sites.

Politicians also actively use social media. Not only do politicians listen to public opinion on social media, but they also use it to persuade voters. Sometimes they seek to frame political issues through social media without relying on traditional mass media. Former US Presidents Trump and Obama, who distributed political content through Twitter, are typical examples.

DOI: 10.4324/9781003143536-5

In summary, social media is a space where many users actively consume news. Even journalists and politicians are involved in the formation of public opinion on social media in various ways. In addition, tweets are sent by the users' own will. Therefore, they are messages written without the presumption that they will be used for academic research and analysis. Thus, we believe that they are closer to public opinion expressed in a natural situation. Therefore, it would be meaningful to analyze what is written on social media to understand public opinion in society as a whole.

Conflicts between Korea and Japan appeared in the media

Social media is a politically polarized space. In 2019, the Knight Foundation published a study conducted by Freelon that analyzed the political tendencies of Twitter users (Freelon, 2019). Freelon showed that the Twitter space of the US is dominated by the moderate left and the far right, and the media vary according to political orientation.

Polarization in social media is not limited to the United States. The case of public opinion concerning the conflict between Korea and Japan is more complicated because the national sentiment of the two countries toward each other is deteriorating. Like many neighboring countries, Korea and Japan have had long-running conflicts over their history and territorial issues. In particular, the deepening conflict from 2018 between Japan and Korea over the issue of forced conscription in World War II continues to worsen even today in 2021. The mass media in both countries have widely reported on this issue with great interest. Moreover, in many countries, a nationalistic bias has been observed in the mass media.

However, in Korea, another variable called "partisan reporting" caused by a conflict between the extreme left and extreme right plays a large role. According to Kim and Lim (2009), who analyzed news reports on the Korean government's media policy and media relations, Korean newspapers showed a clear difference in their reporting attitude as the government's political orientation changed owing to a change of government. In other words, each newspaper advocated for a government similar to its political orientation and criticized those with other political orientations. In reports on North Korea, newspapers in Korea used interviewees to fit the ideological slant of their articles (Kim & Noh, 2011). In addition, in reports that convey scientific information, interviewees were selected according to the political orientation of the media outlet (Lee & Koh, 2009). In Korea, the political orientation of newspapers can be said to influence reporting across many fields.

In the same context, a study analyzing Korean news reports on conflicts between Korea and Japan (Park & Chung, 2020) noted that in contrast to expectations of overly nationalistic media reports, the tendency to make partisan reports based on the network's political stance was obvious. Ogata (2020), in a comparative analysis of Korean and Japanese news reports, also mentioned that regardless of their tone, all Japanese media pointed out the Korean government's faults, while the Korean media tended to criticize according to their political orientation. Specifically, he noted that conservative media outlets took a critical tone of their government led by President Moon Jae-in, who has a progressive tendency. According to Ogata, *The Hankyoreh*, Korea's leading progressive newspaper, completely supported the Moon government's hardline policy against Japan. In other words, in Korea, political interests tend to outweigh nationalism. Because these results are from an analysis of mass news reports, this study attempts to analyze whether the same phenomenon is apparent in social media. In addition, it is worth noting that previous studies have revealed a generally "left-leaning" political orientation among Korean Twitter users. President Moon was elected with strong support from liberals, and it is necessary to consider the characteristics of the Korean media environment, where they are particularly common on Twitter (Hahn, 2013).

This paper attempts to examine whether Japan and Korea have polarized political opinions over the conflicts between the two countries. In general, it is considered that Japan is less polarized than the United States. In particular, there is a view that Japan has no culture of expressing political opinions directly, and the majority of the public remains silent even during major political debates (Hayashi, 2020). According to an analysis of news audience fragmentation in the Japanese Twittersphere using follow relationships, texts of tweets, and surveys (Kobayashi et al., 2019), ideological audience fragmentation is limited. Kobayashi et al. (2019) maintained that fragmentation is only observed among a few media accounts with small numbers of ideologically distinct followers.

More specifically, we analyze how opinions were formed on Twitter concerning this trade dispute between Japan and Korea. To help the reader understand our results, a summary of the background of this dispute is as follows. Japan and Korea, which have often been at odds over their colonial past and territorial disputes, have escalated their mutual animosity owing to an economic conflict sparked by historical issues that arose in 2018 and 2019. Several experts and media in Japan and Korea have described their current relations as the worst since World War II. Specifically, the dispute between the two countries was aggravated by a Korean Supreme Court ruling in October 2018 that a Japanese company should compensate Korean World War II draftees. Furthermore, relations have deteriorated in earnest since Japan's Ministry of Economy and Industry announced a curb on exports of semiconductor materials to Korea in July 2019. In addition, there was a boycott of Japanese products in Korea, and the Korean government announced that it would not renew the General Security of Military Information Agreement (GSOMIA) with Japan.

Research design

Data for this study were collected as follows. First, we set keywords related to this conflict such as "Abe," "Moon Jae-in," "South Korea," "semiconductors," "export sanctions," "export restrictions," "forced labor," "comfort women," and translated them into the Japanese and Korean languages. Based on these keywords, tweets were collected using Twitter API for about six weeks from June 26 to August 5, as the conflict between Korea and Japan had peaked around July 2019. As a result, two sets of data were created: 17 million Japanese tweets and 4.8 million Korean tweets. The difference in numbers seems to reflect the numbers of Twitter users in the respective countries. According to a 2021 survey conducted by the global data research firm Statista, there are about 50 million Twitter users in Japan and 5 million in Korea (Tankovska, 2021).

We first analyzed the overall retweet relationship through network analysis using Python, which we named a *retweet network*. In addition, we found a central group in the retweet network through the clustering process. We then analyzed which words were mainly used by each group, which we would call a *co-occurrence word network*. In addition, we analyzed which mass media outlet's news was most commonly cited by members of the retweet network to examine the relationship between social media users and mass media sources.

To summarize previous research, serious polarization of political opinion does not occur in Japan (Hayashi, 2020; Kobayashi et al., 2019), while in South Korea it is widespread (Kim & Lim, 2009; Kim & Noh, 2011; Lee & Koh, 2009; Park & Chung, 2020). There also seems to be growing hostility between the citizens of Korea and Japan (Ogata, 2020). Based on the above findings, we pose the following research questions.

1 What is the difference between the two countries' retweet networks concerning the conflict between Korea and Japan?
2 What is the relationship between the political leanings of Korean and Japanese Twitter users and those of the mass media sources they cite?

The first research question concerns the structural characteristics of public opinion in social media. In particular, we focused on identifying a small number of users with great influence, i.e., opinion leaders. This is because Twitter is known to be a space where there is a diffusion of secondary information by opinion leaders, described by Katz and Lazarsfeld (1955) as the Two-Step Flow Model. The Two-Step Flow Model, which explains the phenomenon whereby a small number of influential opinion leaders have many followers and strongly influence public opinion, has been identified on Twitter in Korea (Lee, Cha, & Yang, 2011). Therefore, identifying the opinion leaders and the structure around them is essential to understand the characteristics of overall public opinion. For example, by analyzing the retweet networks, we can probe whether opinion leaders in Japan and Korea are nationalistic or politically divided.

The second research question is about the relationship between the political groups identified on Twitter and their references to mass media sources. According to previous studies, it is known that an independent agenda, different from those of the mass media networks, prevails on Twitter (Hwang, 2012; Kwak et al., 2010). In other words, information edited by mass media outlets is not unilaterally delivered via Twitter, but users deliberately select and intensively exchange it so that it attracts attention. In short, we sought to discover which users retweet other's tweets on Twitter, what public opinion was revealed, and which media news sources were most often cited. To facilitate the analysis, 50,000 tweets were randomly extracted from each set.

Results: contrast between a sharp societal division in Japan and a single voice in Korea

Retweet network

Let us first consider the overall structure of the retweet networks in Japan and Korea. As described above, 17 million Japanese language and 4.8 million Korean language tweets were collected, 50,000 were randomly selected and analyzed, and this random sampling was applied equally to all the following graphs.

First, the Japanese data from July show a total of 37,981 accounts in the retweet network. Clustering with Python and visualization through Cytoscape shows two clusters. Furthermore, we selected the top 20 accounts based on the number of retweets, considering the importance of the opinion leader. In addition, from reading the content of tweets, we colored accounts that are critical of Korea red and those critical of Japanese Prime Minister blue. This means that the main interests of the two groups were different, as described below. The larger the circle, the more tweets posted by the account were retweeted. The closer the circles, the more users they share. The results are shown in Figure 5.1.

Figure 5.1 shows two large groups in the Japanese retweet network. In the blue group on the left, many users were critical of former Japanese

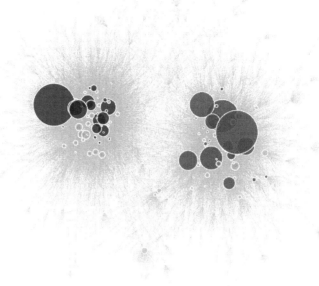

Figure 5.1 Japanese retweet networks.

Prime Minister Shinzo Abe. Moreover, the most retweeted accounts in the group belonged to a famous blogger (http://kikko.cocolog-nifty.com/), who also mainly expressed critical opinions of the Abe government. Given the political landscape of Japan, where the ruling party and Abe rely on the support of the conservative group, we can assume that these users have a relatively liberal political orientation.

In contrast, users in the red group on the right were mainly critical of Korea. The most retweeted account was from a site widely known for its extreme-right tendencies (https://anonymous-post.mobi/). The group also included several conservative politicians from the ruling party, and the Sankei Shimbun, widely known for its conservative tone. From a political perspective, the users can be described as conservative.

In addition, we selected the 20 most retweeted users from the entire network, who can be called opinion leaders, and counted them based on their political orientation. From the tweets sent, accounts critical of Abe were classified as the liberal group, and accounts criticizing Korea were classified as the conservative group. As a result, half the space was occupied by 10 liberal accounts and half by 10 conservative accounts.

Next, let us examine the results of an analysis of Korean tweets. As for Japan, 50,000 cases were randomly selected and analyzed, and 35,266

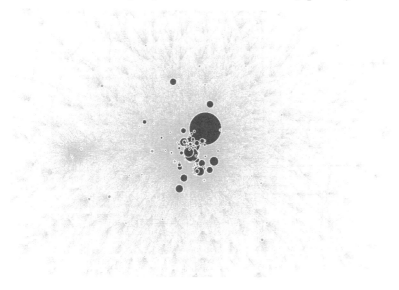

Figure 5.2 Korean retweet networks.

accounts were in the Retweet Network. Only one purple group was observed, as shown in Figure 5.2. The accounts in this group were all strongly critical of Japan and actively supported President Moon. Based on the number of retweets, the first place was held by the official Blue House account, and the second to fifth places were all held by ardent supporters of President Moon. All 20 of the most frequently retweeted users either supported Moon or criticized his opponents. This result can be said to be unusual in Korea, which is known to have strong political polarization, such as the sharp conflict between progressive and conservative forces on many social issues. Admittedly, as mentioned above, it should be remembered that there are many liberal users in the Korean Twitter space.

So far, we have examined the overall structure of retweet networks and the characteristics of their members. From now on, to understand each group better, we consider the most frequently used words within the groups and their combinations in sentences.

Co-occurrence network of words

The words frequently used by the Japanese blue liberal group are shown in Figure 5.3. There are many criticisms of the government, the prime minister, and the ruling party. In addition, words such as "constitutional reform" and "tax increase" are also conspicuous, related to major policies

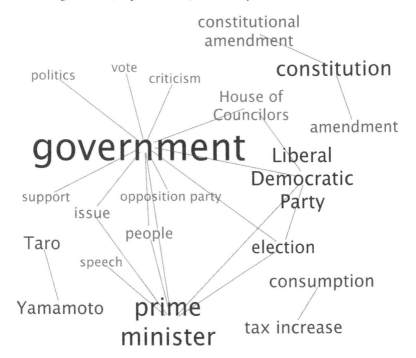

Figure 5.3 Co-occurrence network of the Japanese liberal group.

of the Abe government at the time. "Taro Yamamoto," located at the bottom left, is the name of a politician who received attention for an anti-Abe slogan. Overall, criticism of the Abe regime stands out rather than the conflict between Korea and Japan.

On the other hand, the Japanese conservative group was mainly interested in the conflict between Japan and Korea. Words such as "strengthening," "treatment," "boycott," "(forced) draftee," and "white (list)" were mainly used, and these are key words related to the conflict. Based on this, Figure 5.4 shows many opinions within the conservative group that the Japanese government should respond more strongly and criticizing Korea's response. The term "internet reaction" is frequently added to titles of articles on the right-wing site. For example:

> The Korean government has another excuse … "The discrepancy in statistics of hydrogen fluoride is due to the return of defective products." ~*Internet reaction* "Returned goods! LOL Defective as many as 30%? LOL," "If so, you should have submitted the record of returned goods from the beginning LOL," "Do they really believe returned goods will be removed from the shipment records?"

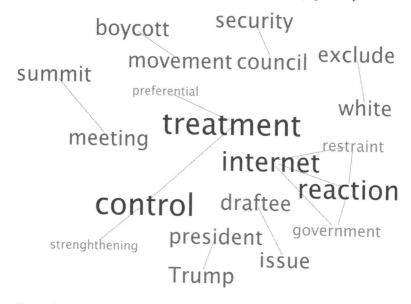

Figure 5.4 Co-occurrence network of the Japanese conservative group.

Figure 5.5 shows that in the Korean set, many terms were used to defend the position of the Korean government or to criticize Japan. Among them, the word "indigenous Japanese raiders" is a profane word for "a person who lives in Korea but takes a position similar to the Japanese," and is used to criticize Koreans who take the side of Japan. The Daum portal ranks second in usage rate in Korea and is known to be widely used by progressive accounts.

This result may be criticized for a lack of representativeness of data because it has been alleged that Korean Twitter users have a leftist bias and tend to support President Moon. With this in mind, we decided to find another analysis target for comparison.

We chose "Naver," the number one portal in Korea. Naver, which boasts an overwhelming use rate in Korea, is known to be a mixture of news favoring both left and right owing to a large number of users. Through the *Ranking News Service* provided by Naver, we selected 32 popular articles related to the Korea–Japan conflict. We then collected the comments on each article, and a dataset of 56,831 comments was created. The co-occurrence word network created from the dataset is as follows. Words such as "we," "people," "country," "forced draft," and "indigenous Japanese raiders" stand out. Overall, the results are not very different from those of the Korean tweet analysis. They also suggest that nationalism is reflected more strongly than political orientation.

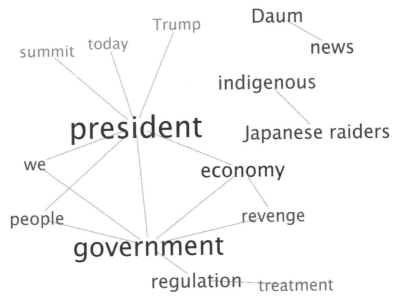

Figure 5.5 Co-occurrence network of Korean tweets.

Frequently cited media sources in tweets

To provide a deeper understanding, the URLs included in the tweet messages were extracted and analyzed to determine which media sources were frequently cited by each group. According to Table 5.1, as may be expected, Japanese liberal groups primarily cited mass media sources with liberal tendencies (blue), while conservative groups cited those known to be conservative (red). To elaborate on the colored media, LITERA is a news site featuring critical news about Japan's ruling party, the Liberal Democratic Party, and its politicians, former Prime Minister Abe and Prime Minister Suga. Mainichi Shimbun is one of Japan's five major national newspapers, and it is known for its center-left tendency and relatively critical stance in relation to Abe. Nikkan Gendai is a tabloid evening magazine that is critical of the Liberal Democratic Party. Meanwhile, the Sankei Shimbun, which is most frequently cited by the Japanese conservative group, is famous for its conservative tendencies, as mentioned above. Zakzak, in second place, is an online version of a tabloid published by the same affiliate group as the Sankei Shimbun. The Japanese conservative group also cited articles from conservative Korean mass media outlets (shown in pink). Chosun Ilbo (www.chosunonline.com) and JoongAng Ilbo (s.japanese.joins.com) are two of Korea's three major conservative media outlets.

Table 5.1 Media cited by the Japanese liberal and conservative groups

Rank	Liberal group	Conservative group
1	lite-ra.com	www.sankei.com
2	mainichi.jp	www.zakzak.co.jp
3	news.livedoor.com	www.recordchina.co.jp
4	www.nikkan-gendai.com	www.chosunonline.com
5	gendai.ismedia.jp	www.news-postseven.com
6	jp.reuters.com	special.sankei.com
7	www.sankei.com	s.japanese.joins.com
8	www.nikkei.com	blog.goo.ne.jp
9	www.bloomberg.com	jp.yna.co.kr
10	news.yahoo.co.jp	tsuisoku.com

Table 5.2 shows that Korean users mainly cited portals and mass media outlets known to reflect similar views to those of the Twitter users toward the Moon government (purple color). As mentioned above, Daum is the second-largest portal in Korea, and it is known to have fewer but more progressive users than Naver, which is the leading portal. However, as shown in Figure 5.6, Naver, which is known to have both liberal and conservative readers, was not very different in that public opinion criticizing Japan and supporting President Moon appeared to be dominant. Meanwhile, the JoongAng Ilbo, which is known to reflect views opposing the Moon government—that is, a conservative tendency—was also included in the top ranks.

Validation of persistence of retweet network analysis results

We further analyzed data from August to December to confirm that the results of the retweet network analysis were not limited to July. Figure 5.7 shows the results, and the retweet network was consistently divided into two groups. A total of 19.4 million tweets were collected in August, 13.6 million in September, 8.9 million in October, 13.6 million in November,

Table 5.2 Media cited by Korean Twitter users

Rank	Anti-Japan and pro-moon group
	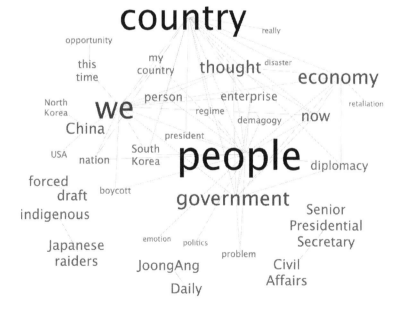
1	news.v.daum.net
2	www.facebook.com
3	m.insight.co.kr
4	news.joins.com
5	n.news.naver.com
6	m.wikitree.co.kr
7	www.vop.co.kr
8	www.youtube.com
9	entertain.v.daum.net
10	news.kbs.co.kr

Figure 5.6 Co-occurrence network of comments from Korean portal sites.

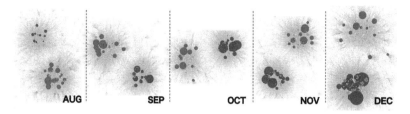

Figure 5.7 Japanese retweet networks from August to December 2019.

and 9 million in December. As in the previous analysis, 50,000 tweets for each period were randomly selected. In addition, 39,884 accounts were in the retweet network in August, 38,316 in September, 38,957 in October, 39,134 in November, and 35,764 in December.

What about Korea? We analyzed the data from August to December as in Japan, but there was a limitation in that the number of tweets decreased sharply from September. Accordingly, from September to December, only the top 10 accounts were colored. The number of collected tweets was 3.79 million in August, 20,257 in September, 24,635 in October, 124,938 in November, and 8,829 in December. In August and November, which exceeded 50,000 tweets, 50,000 were randomly selected, and in September, October, and December, all tweets were analyzed. Figure 5.8 shows the results. The purple accounts are those that supported Korea's President Moon or blamed Japan. This finding can be interpreted to indicate that a single public opinion of a rather closed character was formed. This is generally because only one group of critics of Japan was found who defended their own government's policy. Admittedly, this may be attributed to the overall leftist bias of Korean Twitter users, but it is worth noting that we found no groups with minority opinions. In other words, it was difficult to find any users demanding improvement in relations with Japan or pointing out the limitations of government policies, which seems quite extraordinary considering the political polarization of Korean society. In other words, in Korea, liberals and conservatives tend to confront

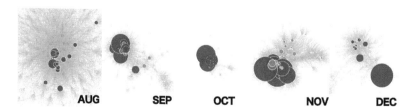

Figure 5.8 Korean retweet networks from August to December 2019.

on most social issues, but regarding conflict with Japan, the opinions of the left and right are not very different. In this regard, although it is difficult to draw conclusions from the results of this paper alone, it can be expected that a "spiral of silence" is taking place. The term "spiral of silence" refers to the process whereby people with minority opinions fear isolation and gradually refrain from expressing their opinions publicly. Alternatively, this may be due to the consolidated antipathy against Japan that is prevalent in Korea because of historical conflicts. Further research is needed to learn whether a spiral of silence drives the seeming homogeneity of opinion in Korea.

Continuity of the accounts

We also analyzed the rate at which the same account continues to tweet and the rate of new arrivals between August and December. In other words, we analyzed the continuity of accounts in relation to the collected data set. All the collected data were analyzed, not just 50,000 random selections. Figure 5.9 shows the percentage of accounts collected in September, October, November, and December that were also collected in August.

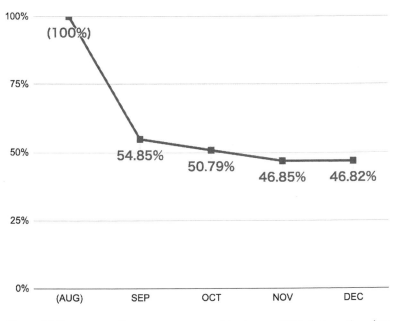

Figure 5.9 Percentage of accounts represented in August 2019 that continued to tweet in September, October, November, and December.

Thus, the result shows how many accounts were continuously retweeting. Of the accounts confirmed in August, 650,839 out of 1,186,476, or 54%, were confirmed to be active in September. In addition, of the 922,886 accounts confirmed in December, 432,128 were also confirmed in August, or 46%. These results indicate that about half of the accounts remained active in tweeting about the Japan–Korea relationship.

Interactions between conservative and liberal groups in Japan

Exchanges within each group were more active than exchanges between liberal and conservative groups (Figure 5.10). The lines shown in Figure 5.10 represent retweet relationships and a node is an account. It can be seen that there is little exchange between the liberal and conservative groups. This means that retweets were mostly between people with similar opinions. The situation in which communication occurs only within a closed space is called the "echo chamber" phenomenon, and there is room for interpretation of this result in connection with this concept. Our findings are in line with those from a previous study of political polarization on Twitter in the US, in which the authors argue that ideologically opposed users very rarely share information from across the divide with other members of their communities (Conover et al., 2011).

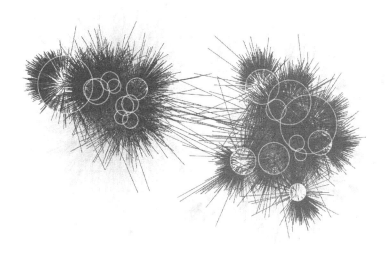

Figure 5.10 Relations in the Japanese retweet networks (July).

Conclusion

We analyzed the differences and commonalities of Japanese and Korean public opinion on Twitter. First, to answer the first research question, "What is the difference between the two countries' retweet networks concerning the conflict between Korea and Japan?" Japan is largely divided into two groups according to political orientation, while only one aggregated group was observed in Korea. In Japan, the liberal group, dominated by critics of the Abe government, and the conservative group generally critical of Korea, expressed different opinions. Considering that this divergence of opinions remained steady not only in July but also from August to December (Figure 5.7), it can be stated that the opinions of Japanese Twitter users on the conflict with Korea are consistently divided. In particular, this result differs from those of previous studies, which reported that in Japan, the public tended not to express political opinions, and political polarization in the Twittersphere was also limited. In other words, this study can be said to have discovered a new aspect of public opinion in Japanese social media. In the Korean case, consistent with the results of previous studies, it was confirmed that no particular polarization of public opinion appears because this issue relates to a conflict with Japan.

As for the second research question, "What is the relationship between the political leanings of Korean and Japanese Twitter users and those of the mass media sources they cite?" as expected, many users cited news from mass media or portal sites with similar political leanings to their own. Rather than interacting with people with opinions contrary to their own, it can be deduced that people with similar political leanings share opinions by using media sources with similar political leanings to their own. It is also worth noting that this phenomenon was commonly observed in both Korea and Japan.

The relationship between Korea and Japan is an important issue in that it could have a significant impact on peace in East Asia. Given its geographical proximity to China, Russia, and North Korea, the deterioration of this relationship could cast a dark cloud over the security and peace of the entire East Asian region. Owing to the trade dispute in 2019 that was the subject of analysis in this study, controversy over the abolition of the GSOMIA between Korea and Japan also arose. That is, a trade dispute created by national sentiment led to security issues.

The relationship between the two countries is still deteriorating in 2021, but experts argue that it could change with the inauguration of US President Biden, who emphasizes the US–Japan–Korea alliance. Indeed, President Moon of Korea began to take an appeasing attitude toward Japan after Biden's inauguration. Moreover, Japan hopes to improve relations with North Korea with the Tokyo Olympics scheduled for July 2021. Therefore, if Korea mediates in this process, there is also room for improvement in Japan–Korea relations. However, given the political leadership in Japan and Korea, there is also skepticism concerning the improvement of relations in the short term. In Korea, as of March 2021, President Moon has only one year left in office, and Japanese Prime Minister Suga is also experiencing a political crisis with low approval ratings.

Japan and Korea's actions will continue to be observed on social media. In 2021, there are notable variables such as the Tokyo Olympics, North Korea, and Biden. Therefore, the online responses to the Japan–Korea relationship are likely to change dynamically and a comparison with 2019 results could provide meaningful insights. Although this study only analyzed Twitter, it would be possible to conduct an analysis in greater depth if various data sources such as YouTube, news articles, and surveys were used.

In addition, it is important to continue to track and analyze the reactions of users to news reports and social media for improving the relationship between the two countries. This is because to understand the positions of people with different political positions, we must first recognize how our values differ. Furthermore, we believe that recognizing each other's values and making efforts to communicate are the first steps toward overcoming the closed nationalism emerging in many countries.

References

Conover, M., Ratkiewicz, J., Francisco, M., Gonçalves, B., Menczer, F., & Flammini, A. (2011). Political polarization on Twitter. In *Proceedings of the International AAAI Conference on Web and Social Media, 5*(1), 89–96.

Freelon, D. (2019). Tweeting Left, Right & Center: How Users and Attention Are Distributed across Twitter. Retrieved Mar 23, 2021, from https://knightfoundation.org/articles/polarization-in-the-twittersphere-what-86-million-tweets-reveal-about-the-political-makeup-of-american-twitter-users-and-how-they-engage-with-news

Hahn, K. (2013). A Test of Representativeness and Polarization in Twitter Followership: A Cross-National Assessment of Legislators' Twitter Followers in the US and South Korea. *Journal of Cyber Communication Academic Society, 30*(1), 295–336.

Hayashi, K. (2020). The Silent Public in a Liberal State: Challenges for Japan's Journalism in the Age of the Internet. In *The Crisis of Liberal Internationalism: Japan and the World Order.* Edited by Yoichi Funabashi and G. John Ikenberry. Brookings Institution Press. Washington. D.C. 325–358.

Hwang, Y. (2012). A Comparative Study of Information Diffusion between Conservative and Liberal Media. *Korean Journal of Journalism & Communication Studies, 56*(5), 350–372.

Katz, E., & Lazarsfeld, P. F. (1955). *Personal influence: the part played by people in the flow of mass communications.* Free Press. Glencoe, IL.

Kim, H. (2013). Message Attributes, Consequences, and Values in Retweet Behavior: Based on Laddering Method. *The Journal of the Korea Contents Association, 13*(3), 131–140. doi:10.5392/JKCA.2013.13.03.131

Kim, K. & Noh, G. (2011). A Comparative Study of News Reporting about North Korea in Newspapers in South Korea. *Korean Journal of Journalism & Communication Studies, 55*(1), 361–387.

Kim, Y. & Lim, Y. (2009). An Analysis of News Reports about Government–Media Relationships and Media Policies: Comparison of News Contents under Noh–Lee Governments. *Korean Journal of Journalism & Communication Studies, 53*(4), 94–115.

Kobayashi, T., Ogawa, Y., Suzuki, T., & Yamamoto, H. (2019). News audience fragmentation in the Japanese Twittersphere. *Asian Journal of Communication, 29*(3), 274–290. doi:10.1080/01292986.2018.1458326

Kwak, H., Lee, C., Park, H., & Moon, S. (2010). What is Twitter, a Social Network or a News Media?. In *Proceedings of the 19th International Conference on World Wide Web.* ACM Press. doi:10.1145/1772690.1772751

Lee, G. & Koh, H. (2009). Korean Newspapers Political Orientation Featuring in US Beef Imports Articles: Analysis of Source Information Valence in Five Newspapers. *Korean Journal of Journalism & Communication Studies, 53*(3), 347–369.

Lee, W., Cha, M., & Yang, H. (2011). Network Properties of Social Media Influentials: Focusing on the Korean Twitter Community. *Journal of Communication Research, 48*(2), 44–79. doi:10.22174/jcr.2011.48.2.44

Newman, N., Fletcher, R., Schulz, A., Andi, S., & Nielsen, R. K. (2020). *Digital News Report 2020.* Reuters Institute. Oxford. Retrieved Mar 23, 2021, from http://www.digitalnewsreport.org/

Ogata, Y. (2020). Cognitive Framing of the Media Regarding Deteriorating Japan–ROK Relations: Focusing on Editorials in Major Japanese and Korean Newspapers in 2019. *The Korean Journal of Japanology, 124*, 191–216. doi:10.15532/kaja.2020.08.124.191

Park, Y. & Chung, J. (2020). How Did the Press Report the Conflict Between Korea and Japan?: Focusing on Framing and Signifying Strategies. *The Journal of the Korea Contents Association, 20*(7), 352–367. doi:10.5392/JKCA.2020.20.07.352

Tankovska, H. (2021). *Leading countries based on number of Twitter users as of January 2021.* Statista. Hamburg. Retrieved Mar 23, 2021, from https://www.statista.com/statistics/242606/number-of-active-twitter-users-in-selected-countries/.

6 Semantic structure of the comfort women issue in Japanese and South Korean newspapers

Yuki Ogawa, Tetsuro Kobayashi

In analyzing public opinion on the issue of conflict between Japan and South Korea (hereafter, Korea), the role played by the media cannot be ignored. The media influence public opinion in various ways, which, in turn, constrains the foreign policy of governments. Politicians and governments are also sensitive to the influence of the media on public opinion, and therefore try to provide information on international issues in a way that is favorable to their positions, which then influences the media's agenda setting. To unravel the complex relationship between public opinion, governments, and the media, it is imperative to analyze how bilateral international conflict issues are reported in each country involved.

Although the effect of the media in directly persuading the public is not necessarily great, the way in which issues are framed in the media is known to have a significant impact on the attribution of responsibility for the problem and the solutions deemed necessary. In his classic study of media framing effects, Iyengar (1991) argues that when media coverage of poverty focuses on specific people suffering from poverty (i.e., episodic framing), the blame for the problem is attributed to those individuals (e.g., bad luck, laziness) and not to society as a whole. In contrast, when thematic framing is used, in which the poverty problem is reported along with the structural background and statistical data, the problem is considered to be one of the whole society and should be actively solved by the government. Thus, in the case of international conflict issues, depending on how the conflict is framed, who should be held responsible and whose and what actions are considered to lead to a solution can be expected to differ significantly.

This framing effect of the media on public opinion is expected to be particularly large in international conflict issues. First, the dispute between nations is typically an unobtrusive issue, which means that most people will not experience it directly. In other words, the source of information on international conflicts is almost exclusively the media. Because the source

DOI: 10.4324/9781003143536-6

of information is limited to the media and is not moderated by direct experience, the effect of the media on public opinion becomes stronger. Second, issues of international conflict are known to be reported in ways that are consistent with each country's national interests. Analyzing how the NATO airstrikes in Kosovo were framed differently by the Chinese and US media, Yang (2003) found that Chinese newspapers framed the airstrikes as an intervention in Yugoslavia's sovereignty and territory, while US newspapers framed them as humanitarian aid to Albanians to stop ethnic cleansing initiated by the Serbs. The fact that newspapers reflect the positions of governments toward airstrikes shows that national interests have a considerable influence on the media frames of newspapers. Third, in recent years, the development of the Internet has made it much easier to read news reports from the other side of the conflict in one's native language. Before the widespread use of the Internet, it was difficult for ordinary Japanese to directly read reports related to the comfort women issue in Korea, but now major South Korean (hereafter, Korean) newspapers, such as Chosun Ilbo and JoongAng Ilbo, have established Japanese language pages and Japanese accounts on social media such as Twitter. With the information obtained from these sources, even Japanese who cannot read Korean can now easily find out how the conflict issue is being reported in Korea. Given that conflict issues tend to be reported in a manner consistent with national interests, it is not difficult to imagine that some Japanese may have a negative impression of the way conflict issues are framed in Korea. This new form of international communication made possible by the Internet is also likely to have an impact on public opinion.

Therefore, it is imperative to analyze the media frames of Japan and Korea in a comparable manner when considering the international conflict issues between the two countries. In this chapter, we examine the differences in media frames through the analysis of newspaper articles from both countries on Japan and Korea's conflict issues. In particular, we focus on the comfort women issue because, along with the Takeshima/Dokdo territorial issue, this has been the most salient dispute between Japan and Korea since the 1990s. Because this study attempts to extract frames by analyzing news articles, it is not possible to analyze the effect of media frames on public opinion. However, it is quite likely that media coverage of the conflict issues between Japan and Korea has a substantial impact on public opinion in each country. For example, Moon and Sung (2006) conducted a survey of 260 Koreans. After reading negative articles about Japan, the participants were asked about their perceptions of Japan and their willingness to purchase Japanese products. The results showed that when they were exposed to negative articles, they became more critical of Japan and more negative about purchasing Japanese products. In other words, exposure to articles critical of Japan led to a more negative perception of Japan. An international conflict is one to which the people of both countries will be paying close attention, but compromise and resolution will be difficult if the two sides view the issue very differently due to different media frames.

Media content analysis of Japan–Korea conflict issues

The content analysis of the media on the conflict issues between Japan and Korea shows that both countries use different frames to report the issues. Furthermore, a comparison of the domestic media in each country suggests that the liberal and conservative media report the issue differently.

In an analysis of Korean domestic media, Lee and Min (2011) analyzed comfort women-related articles from December 2000 to October 2010 in the Chosun Ilbo and Hankyoreh newspapers and found that the frames that appear most often were "sexual slavery by Japan" and "Japan's apology and compensation." Lee, Bae, and Park (2016) analyzed the contents of Chosun Ilbo and Kyunghyang Shinmun from September 2006 to December 2015 and found that news about comfort women issues was the prime element of the conflict. In their analysis, 63% of the articles were found to have a negative tone against Japan, describing Prime Minister Abe's cabinet as the conflict's primary inducer. They also argue that ideological factors accounted for why the Korean reports were not objective and balanced. In contrast, Park and Chung (2020) found that, although Korea is also known for its fierce partisan rivalry between conservative and progressive camps, it does not show partisan reporting when reporting relationship issues with Japan, suggesting that public opinion is generally consolidated over the issues. They argue that this is due to nationalism or patriotism in Korea. Lee (2007) analyzed Japan-related news reports in Korean TV news (KBS, MBC, and SBS) in 2003–2004 and concluded that Korean news reports frame Japan-related news with the tone of "defending South Korea and criticizing Japan" due to past historical issues, with 18% of news positively reported and 33% negatively valenced.

The Japanese media coverage of Japan–Korea conflict issues has been less extensively studied compared with that of the Korean media. However, several studies have highlighted differences in framing in the conservative and liberal Japanese media. Takekawa (2016) argues that, for the liberal Asahi Shimbun, it is crucial for Japan to face up to its wartime aggressions and extend sincere apologies. For the conservative Yomiuri Shimbun and Sankei Shimbun, on the other hand, it is vital to reject unfounded accusations against Imperial Japan and restore its dignity.

Studies that analyze media coverage in Japan and Korea in a comparable manner show that conflict issues are framed differently in the two countries. Oh (2011) found that Korean newspapers tend to employ a morality frame while Japanese newspapers tend to employ a future-oriented frame. Korean newspapers emphasize that Japan has a responsibility to take further actions, such as acknowledging the unfairness of the forced merger between Korea and Japan in 1910. In contrast, Japanese newspapers stress the Japanese government's previous apologies and related efforts to restore the damage. Among the liberal Japanese newspapers, Asahi and Mainichi emphasize the attribution-of-responsibility frame the most, while the conservative Yomiuri emphasizes the future-oriented frame and rarely employs the morality frame. Pak (2016) conducted a content analysis of 384 comfort women-related articles in two Korean newspapers, Chosun Ilbo and Hankyoreh, and in two Japanese newspapers, Yomiuri and Asahi. Applying the framing categories of Semetko and Valkenburg (2000), it was found that Korean articles contained more responsibility frames, while Japanese articles had more conflict frames. Korean newspapers tended to report concisely on events, people, and noteworthy statements (such as gaffes by Japanese politicians), while Japanese newspapers tended to have a more in-depth analysis of the issues (such as background, causes, and effects), expert analysis, and relatively longer articles. Thus, the characteristic of Korean newspapers to report on the comfort women issue in a negative tone by using many episodic frames likely reinforces readers' negative impression of the Japanese government and politicians.

These previous studies suggest that conflict issues in Japan and Korea are reported using different frames in the two countries. However, some limitations of these previous studies remain. The classification of frames varies from study to study, making comparison across multiple studies difficult. For example, Pak (2016) uses three classifications of frames by Semetko and Valkenburg (2000), episodic vs. thematic frames, and positive vs. negative tones. Although these frames have been shown to be useful, it is not clear whether the conflict issues between Japan and Korea are necessarily reported in a manner consistent with these frames. In other words, arbitrariness in predefining the frames before content analysis cannot be ruled out. In addition, all previous studies are based on manual coding. While manual coding of frames by human coders has the advantage of enabling classification based on judgments close to the viewpoint of human readers, in practice, it is difficult to classify a large number of news articles. Moreover, if the frames are complicated, intercoder reliability may be reduced. With predefined frames, the coder is forced to classify the articles into those frames.

With these limitations in mind, this study employs large-scale computational text mining and attempts to analyze the contents with higher comprehensiveness and objectivity than conventional manual coding. We initially extract frames from a large number of news articles without predefining frames. This allows us to analyze frames specific to the Japan–Korea issue, rather than setting frames a priori. In addition, by using computational text mining, we can analyze a massively large volume of news articles compared with previous studies. By including more recent articles than those analyzed in previous studies, we will be able to highlight new developments in the Japan–Korea conflict issue. In particular, the situation surrounding the comfort women issue has changed significantly with the agreement between Japan and Korea at the end of 2015. By including these more recent developments in the analysis, we aim to increase the depth of the frame analysis.

Method

The target of the analysis in this study is limited to newspapers. Although the readership of print newspapers is declining, newspaper articles still reach a broad audience through online news and social media. Therefore, the frames of a newspaper influence public opinion beyond the people who directly subscribe to the newspaper. The leading role that newspapers play in how international conflicts are framed cannot yet be ignored.

We extract frames from a large number of Japanese and Korean newspaper articles using a text mining approach called Word2Vec (Mikolov et al., 2013). This approach has the advantage of being able to computationally extract frames from a large amount of text data, thus enabling a more objective analysis than the existing manual coding of frames. Text mining is used to quantitatively understand the contents of a large amount of document data by obtaining useful information from them. Word2Vec is a text mining technique that can represent the meaning of a word as a vector, and it learns the meaning of a word from the words that appear around it in the text. For example, in Article$_1$ and Article$_2$ in Figure 6.1, the word "aaa" and the word "bbb" have the words "eee," "ccc," "ddd," and "eee" in common adjacent locations. Therefore, it is inferred that "aaa" and "bbb" are words that express similar meanings. In this way, by using the information of word groups appearing around a specific word, it is possible to characterize words by taking into account the contexts of the document, and thus, it is possible to represent words with higher quality than the conventional word vector representation based on the simple occurrence or co-occurrence of words. Word2Vec is applied in chatbots, sentiment analysis, and sentence summarization.

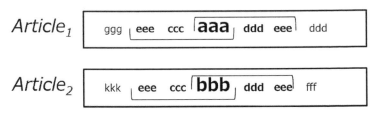

e.g., Similarity of context between Word$_{aaa}$ and Word$_{bbb}$ (window size =3)

Figure 6.1 Generating semantic vectors with Word2Vec.

Frame extraction from newspaper articles using Word2Vec

We attempt to extract the frames of conflict issues by applying Word2Vec to the text data of a large number of newspaper articles from Japan and Korea. The way a certain issue is discussed in newspaper articles varies depending on the country and the media. The issue of comfort women may be discussed with the human rights frame or with a diplomacy frame. Although it is possible to grasp the frames roughly from the differences in the words that appear and the co-occurrence relationships between the words, it is difficult to extract frames properly from simple word occurrences and co-occurrence relationships because there are cases where multiple topics are mixed in an article, or where the context in which the topic is discussed differs even if similar words are used.

Semantic vector representation of words using Word2Vec is useful to address these concerns because it takes into account the information of surrounding words. When the term "comfort women" is converted into a semantic vector using Word2Vec, this vector summarizes the flow of sentences in which the word "comfort women" appears, and thus can be regarded as a vector that captures the context of the topic. Furthermore, by looking at word groups that are similar to this word vector, it allows us to interpret the framing in which the word is used. In the following, we outline the steps of Word2Vec.

First, we use Word2Vec to convert the words in newspaper articles into semantic vectors. This means that the document x word matrix is reduced and converted into multiple vectors consisting of weighted combinations of words (Figure 6.2). Next, based on the similarity between the vectors, we cluster the words that are similar to "comfort women" (Figure 6.3), which identifies the main clusters related to the comfort women issue. Finally, we visualize the relationship between the main cluster of the comfort woman issue and other clusters that are similar to the comfort women cluster in a dendrogram (Figure 6.4). This allows us to identify the frames in which

Count frequency of words in article

Articles \ Words	W_1	W_2	W_3	...	W_m
Article$_1$	10	4	0	3	5
Article$_2$	2	0	0	0	3
Article$_3$	0	7	1	0	0
...	...	...	...	...	...
Article$_n$	4	3	0	0	0

Vectorize words by using **Word2Vec**

Words \ Dimension	X_1	X_2	X_3	...	X_m
Word$_1$	0.3	0.1	0.2	0.4	0.4
Word$_2$	0.2	0.1	0.1	0.4	0.5
Word$_3$	0.9	0.3	0.6	0.1	0.3
...	...	...	...	...	...
Word$_m$	0.8	0.4	0.1	0.2	0.3

Figure 6.2 Semantic vectorization of words in a newspaper article using Word2Vec.

the issue of comfort women is reported in news articles. For example, if the comfort women issue is reported in the diplomacy frame, the comfort women cluster and the cluster related to diplomacy should appear close to each other in the dendrogram. Alternatively, if the comfort women issue is reported in the frame of violation of women's human rights, the cluster related to human rights should appear close to the comfort women cluster in the dendrogram.

Newspaper articles for analysis

Our analysis covers conservative and liberal newspapers in both Japan and Korea. In Japan, the conservative newspaper, Yomiuri, and the liberal newspaper, Asahi, were selected. In Korea, the conservative newspaper, Chosun Ilbo, and the liberal newspaper, Hankyoreh, were targeted. All articles on all pages are included in the analysis. The period covered was six years, from 2011 to 2016. For the Japanese newspaper articles, we used the database sold by each of the newspapers for each year. The Korean newspaper articles were collected by crawling the portal site Naver.[1] The

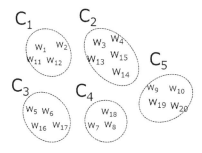

Figure 6.3 Clustering of words.

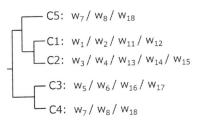

Figure 6.4 Dendrogram of associations between clusters.

number of articles analyzed for each newspaper is shown in Table 6.1. The number of Japanese newspaper articles is generally larger because small columns were also counted.

The period 2011–2016 includes events such as the landing of President Lee Myung-bak on Takeshima/Dokdo in 2012, frequent references to the comfort women issue by Japanese politicians in 2013, and the Japan–Korea agreement on the comfort women issue in 2015; thus, the articles include the period when Japan and Korea's respective media covered the conflict issues extensively.

Results

First, we analyzed the percentage of articles in which the word "comfort women" appeared in each newspaper article to elucidate when the comfort women issue was intensively covered in Japanese and Korean newspapers (Figure 6.5). It can be seen that many articles containing the word "comfort women" in Japanese newspapers were published during the period of former Osaka Mayor Hashimoto's statements on comfort women in 2013, the verification of the Kono statement in 2014, the issue of the retraction of comfort women articles by Asahi in 2014, and the Japan–Korea agreement on the comfort women issue in 2015. No major differences were found between Yomiuri and Asahi in terms of the trends, although the

Table 6.1 Total number of newspaper articles for analysis by year

Number of newspaper articles		2011	2012	2013	2014	2015	2016
Japan	Yomiuri (Cons.)	2,77,009	2,74,213	2,66,347	2,48,941	2,38,186	2,31,636
	Asahi (Liberal)	1,20,061	1,25,182	1,20,960	1,16,038	1,11,795	1,06,947
Korea	Chosun (Cons.)	58,797	55,748	49,279	46,544	47,433	65,502
	Hankyoreh (Liberal)	29,794	26,474	20,411	18,559	19,871	14,250

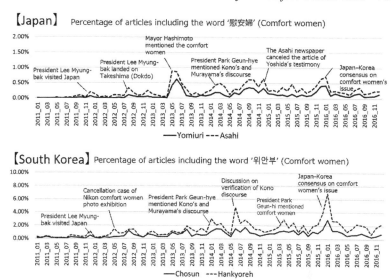

Figure 6.5 Percentage of articles in which the word "comfort women" appears in Japanese and Korean newspaper articles.

percentage of the articles tended to be larger in Asahi than in Yomiuri. On the other hand, Korean newspapers had the most articles containing the word "comfort women" during the period of the Japan–Korea agreement on the comfort women issue in 2015. Former Osaka Mayor Hashimoto's derogatory statements on the comfort women issue in 2013, which were widely covered in Japanese newspapers, were barely covered in Korean newspapers. No major differences were found between Chosun Ilbo and Hankyoreh in terms of the trends, although the percentage of the articles tended to be larger in Hankyoreh than in Chosun Ilbo.

Framing of the comfort women issue in Japanese newspapers

Next, we examine the frames of the comfort women issue from our dendrograms. The dendrogram obtained from the analysis of Japanese newspaper articles is shown in Figure 6.6. The analysis of Yomiuri and Asahi combined ("All" in Figure 6.6) shows that the main cluster of comfort women-related terms includes the Kono statement, the Japanese military comfort women issue, historical awareness, and the Korean people. This cluster is shown in red in the dendrogram on the right of Figure 6.6. The clusters adjacent to the comfort women cluster in the dendrogram are mostly related to law and court cases. In addition, clusters related to war

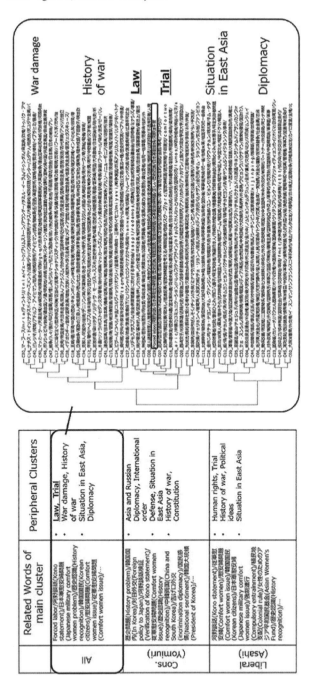

Figure 6.6 Main cluster of comfort women and the dendrogram of related clusters in Japanese newspapers.

damage, history of war, the situation in East Asia, and diplomacy appear around it. From this overall pattern, we interpret the issue of comfort women in Japan as being framed primarily in the context of sexual forced labor. In Japan, because coercion in the recruitment of comfort women tends to be particularly highlighted, the frames related to legal issues and court cases are frequently used. In addition, the clusters on the situation in East Asia and diplomacy also appear in the vicinity of the comfort women cluster, indicating that the issue is framed as a diplomatic issue in East Asia in addition to the forced labor frame.

Analyzing Yomiuri and Asahi separately, we see that they use different frames. Yomiuri's main cluster on comfort women includes "China and South Korea," indicating that the comfort women issue is positioned as one of the points of contention in East Asian diplomacy, including China. It also contains words that negatively portray the Korean government's position, as seen in the phrase "incrimination diplomacy." Furthermore, clusters related to diplomacy with Russia and security in East Asia also appear in the clusters surrounding the comfort women cluster, confirming the tendency for the comfort women issue to be framed as a diplomatic issue. On the other hand, Asahi's main cluster on comfort women includes words that are not found in Yomiuri, such as "colonial rule" and "Asian Women's Fund." These words indicate that Asahi has a relatively strong tendency to frame the comfort women issue from the perspective of war responsibility and its reparation. Clusters related to human rights and war history also appear in the clusters surrounding the comfort women cluster, indicating that Asahi frames the comfort women issue as part of a broader human rights issue rather than as a diplomatic or security issue.

Framing of the comfort women issue in Korean newspapers

The dendrogram obtained from analysis of Korean newspaper articles is shown in Figure 6.7. Analysis of Chosun Ilbo and Hankyoreh combined ("All" in Figure 6.7) shows that the main cluster of comfort women includes war crimes, sexual slavery, and apology. This cluster is shown in red in the dendrogram on the right of Figure 6.7. The cluster adjacent to the comfort women cluster in the dendrogram shows that there are clusters related to historical issues, independence movements, and democratization movements. In addition, clusters related to war damage, criticism, and the situation in East Asia appear around the cluster. From this overall pattern, it can be interpreted that the comfort women issue in Korean newspapers is framed in the context of Japan's war crimes. Notably, the comfort women issue is framed as an issue related to independence from Japanese colonial rule and the subsequent democratization. Unlike in the

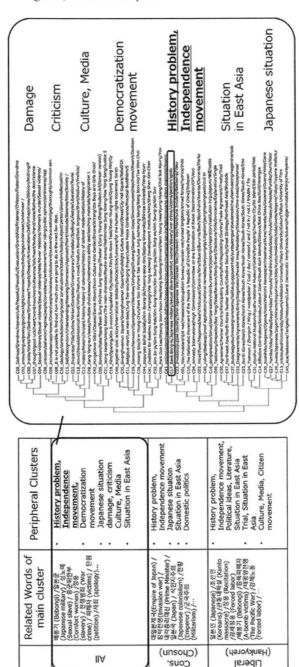

Figure 6.7 Main cluster of comfort women and the dendrogram of related clusters in Korean newspapers.

Japanese press, there was little framing of the issue to position it as part of East Asian diplomacy.

An analysis of Chosun Ilbo and Hankyoreh separately does not reveal any major differences between them. Both newspapers frame the comfort women issue as a historical problem and war crime, and report from the perspective of Japanese colonialism, militarism, aggression, and forced labor. The similarity between Chosun Ilbo and Hankyoreh is in contrast to the differences in framing found between the conservative Yomiuri and the liberal Asahi in Japan. The difference between the two countries reflects the fact that there is a broad domestic agreement in Korea on the framing of the comfort women issue, that is, as an issue of dispute with Japan.

Longitudinal changes in the framing of the comfort women issue

Finally, we analyze how the framing of the comfort women issue has changed between 2011 and 2016 in Japan and Korea. Figure 6.8 shows the main comfort women clusters for each year in each country. The analyses combine the two newspapers in each country.

It is noteworthy that the Japanese newspapers included the Takeshima/ Dokdo issue within the main cluster of the comfort women issue in 2011 and 2012. In other words, the comfort women issue was lumped together with territorial issues and framed as a diplomatic dispute between Japan and Korea. This change may have been influenced by President Lee Myung-bak's landing on Takeshima/Dokdo in August 2012. The association of the comfort women issue with the territorial issue is also consistent with the emergence of clusters related to the East Asian situation and security in the peripheral clusters. In 2013, however, there was an increase in the association with words related to the Yasukuni Shrine issue and Class A war criminals, and clusters related to law and court cases emerged in the surrounding clusters. This trend partially reflects the fact that the statement made by former Osaka Mayor Toru Hashimoto that "the comfort women system was necessary" invoked a partisan conflict in May 2013. In 2014, the retraction of articles on the comfort women issue by Asahi was a salient news story, and this is reflected in the word list of the comfort women main cluster. In 2015, the framing of the issue as a diplomatic issue was foregrounded, reflecting the Japan–Korea agreement at the end of the year. Reflecting this change, frames related to East Asian affairs and diplomacy began to appear in the peripheral clusters as well. In general, the results suggest that the framing of the comfort women issue in Japanese newspapers has fluctuated longitudinally. The comfort women

		2011	2012	2013	2014	2015	2016
Japan	Related Words of main cluster	独島·大統領府(Korean presidential office)/独島問題(Korea side)/竹島問題(Takeshima issue)/...	竹島(Takeshima)/領有権(Territorial rights)/国際問題(International law)/韓国領有権問題(Territorial issue)/竹島問題(Territorial issue)/...	靖国神社(Yasukuni Shrine)/靖国(Yasukuni)/参拝問題(Worship)/極東国際軍事裁判(Far East International Military Trial)/首相(Prime Minister)/...	河野談話(cono)/吉田証言(Yoshida Testimony)/論点整理(Compulsory entrainment)/すり替え(Exchange)/強制連行(Changing points of argument)/従軍慰安婦 誤魔化えた(Twist of comfort women problem)/事実(fact)/...	慰安婦問題(Comfort women issue)/日韓問題(History problem)/朴大統領(President Park Geun)/外交問題(Diplomatic issue)/日韓(Japan and South Korea)/...	忠清南道(Chungcheongnam-do)/トーク?(Dokdo)/盧武鉉(Roh Tae)/日韓慰安婦問題交渉(Embassy of Japan in Korea)/慰安婦問題(Korea)/慰安婦問題(Korea name)/...
	Peripheral Clusters	• Situation in East Asia, East Asian diplomacy • Defense, Security, world situation • Domestic politics, Trial • Ideology, Literature, War history, International order	• Security, East Asian affairs, defense • War history, Ideology, culture • International Peace, Trial, Domestic Politics, Law, Constitution	• Law, Trial, Constitution • Political ideas • East Asia situation, International order	• Judgment, Responsibility, Verification • East Asia situation, Education, Culture, War history, Domestic politics	• East Asian diplomacy, situation in East Asia • War damage, History, Damage • Thought, Culture, Education • Political criticism, Law, Trial	• East Asia situation, East Asia and Russia diplomacy, Security • Trial, Human right, Constitution • Literature, War history
South Korea	Related Words of main cluster	실효지배(Effective control)/독도(Patrol boat)/독도영유권(Dokdo Island)/독도 문제(Territorial dispute)/영유(Possession)/센카쿠열도(Senkaku Islands)/영유권/영토(territory)/무라야마담화(Kono statement)/센카쿠(Senkaku)/독도문제(A crash case)/...	영유권(reflux)/야스쿠니(Goyo)/무라야마담화(Militarism)/쿠릴 열도(Kuril Islands)/독도영유권(South Kuril Islands)/다케시마(Takeshima)/영토(annexation)/침략(aggression)/영토분쟁(Invasion war)/무라야마담화(Kono statement)/군함도(Gunkan)/러일전쟁(Russo-Japanese War)/천황(Emperor)/...	조선인(Korean)/독도(Dokdo)/담화(Recitation)/일본군(The Japanese army)/위안부(Sexual slave)/일본(An atom)/간(Kanto)/정부(aggression)/일본정부(Japanese government)/조선여자근로정신대(Women's volunteer corps)/태평양전쟁(The Pacific War)/...	침략전쟁(Invasion war)/종군(Japan)/군국주의(Militarism)/종군위안부(Comfort women)/보수(conservative)/침략(aggression)/평화헌법(Peace Constitution)/침략전쟁(Aggressionism)/야스쿠니(conservatism swing)/야스쿠니신사(Yasukuni Shrine)/...	강제노동(Forced labor)/일본군(The Japanese army)/강제징용(Forced labor)/일본군위안부(Japanese military comfort women)/조선인(The Korean)/정신대(The Korean Drafted for Military Sexual Slavery by Japan)/군위안부(Kim Dong Dong)/위령탑(Cenotaph)/성노예(Sexual slave)/...	사죄(apology)/성노예(Sexual slave)/일본정부(Japanese government)/일본군(The Japanese army)/일본군(aggression)/군(Army)/수상(Prime Minister)/과거(An atom)/전범(War crime)/정신대(Kim Dong Dong)/군위안부(Kim Dong Dong)/히로시마(Hiroshima)/일본국(Japanese state)/위안부(Comfort women)/...
	Peripheral Clusters	• East Asia situation, Japanese situation • Law, trial • War history, Independence movement • Life, Culture	• East Asian affairs, Japan situation • Domestic politics, Trial • Diplomacy, History, Culture, Human rights	• Japanese situation, Situation in East Asia • War damage, War History • Human rights, Education, Culture, Media • Domestic politics	• Japan situation, Situation in East Asia, War damage • Ideology, Culture, Media • Domestic politics, Trial	• Japan situation, Independence movement • Culture, Media Education • Trial, Domestic politics, Situation in East Asia	• Japan situation, War, Independence movement, defense education • Citizen movement, Trial Culture, Media, Human rights

Figure 6.8 Longitudinal changes in the framing of the comfort women issue.

issue was sometimes framed as a bilateral dispute combined with territorial disputes; at other times, it was framed as an issue related to domestic partisan conflicts and the credibility of media coverage; and at yet other times, it was framed as one of the diplomatic issues in East Asia. This indicates that the framing of Japan's comfort women coverage is not consistent, and that public opinion is likely to be shaped by the highly relevant framing at any given time.

Next, looking at the changes in the framing of the comfort women issue in Korea, we can see that it has not fluctuated as much as in Japan. In 2011 and 2012, the main cluster of the comfort women issue was related to the Takeshima/Dokdo issue, as in Japan; however, since 2013, it has been consistently framed in relation to Japan's war responsibility, war crimes, and the independence movement from Japanese colonial rule. In the peripheral clusters, human rights, war damage, and war history have also repeatedly appeared, albeit with some fluctuations. As a result, the framing of the comfort women issue in Korea is consistent in relation to Japan's colonial rule and independence from it, war crimes, and human rights violations. This consistency of framing in Korea may be related to the fact that Korean public opinion has been consistently critical of the Japanese government's response and continues to demand a sincere apology.

Discussion

This study analyzed how the comfort women issue, a major conflict issue between Japan and Korea, has been framed in both countries through a computational analysis of a large number of newspaper articles from two Japanese and two Korean newspapers from 2011 to 2016.

In general, the framing of the comfort women issue in Japanese newspapers was not consistent. In addition to the war responsibility frame, such as human rights violations and forced labor, a variety of frames were used, including the frame as one of the points of contention in East Asian diplomacy, including China and Russia, and legal frames such as compensation and court cases. In addition, these frames tend to change longitudinally and sometimes frames as domestic issues emerged, as in the case of former Osaka Mayor Hashimoto's statements and the retraction of the Asahi article. Furthermore, we found a marked difference in framing between the conservative Yomiuri and the liberal Asahi, with the former more likely to use the East Asian diplomatic frame and the latter the human rights frame. These ideological differences are consistent with Pak's (2016) findings. The inconsistent framing of comfort women coverage in Japanese newspapers and the conservative–liberal differences suggest that the comfort women issue is not only a contentious issue with Korea, but is also likely to become a domestic partisan conflict. With conservatives and liberals viewing the comfort women issue from different perspectives, Japan's position would appear to be inconsistent from Korea's perspective. Moreover, if the comfort women issue is subsumed into domestic partisan conflicts, it will be difficult for the entire country to share the understanding that this is an issue to be tackled as a whole.

In contrast, Korean newspaper reports have consistently framed the comfort women issue as a Japanese war crime. There is a growing trend around the world to consider the comfort women issue as one of the more universal issues of wartime violence that seriously violated women's human rights. The Korean press has reported on the comfort women issue in a frame that is consistent with this global trend, and in this respect, it has adopted a frame that is highly compatible with the Western media that emphasize human rights issues. It is also interesting to note that the comfort women issue has been reported in relation to independence and democratization movements. It can be said that overcoming the comfort women issue is framed as an issue that "should be resolved correctly" in the context of Korea's history of independence from Japanese colonial rule and subsequent democratization from military rule. This tendency of framing the comfort women issue as Japan's war responsibility has shown a clearer longitudinal consistency than in Japan, although there were some fluctuations. Furthermore, in contrast to Japan, there is no significant difference in framing between the conservative Chosun Ilbo and the liberal Hankyoreh. Korea is experiencing serious ideological conflicts between conservatives and progressives in terms of generations and regions, creating a polarized political situation in which the two camps cannot compromise on a variety of issues. Despite this, the conservative and progressive camps have adopted almost the same frame of reference in reporting on the comfort women issue. This longitudinal consistency in the coverage by Korean newspapers of the comfort women issue and the agreement between conservatives and progressives are likely to be reasons for the strength and consistency of Korean citizens' attitudes on this issue.

To see a certain degree of consensus at the level of public opinion on a contentious international issue like the comfort women issue, it is necessary for the citizens of Japan and Korea to share the same perspective. Otherwise, the arguments of the two sides will not mesh and the debate will remain parallel. If one party to the conflict believes that the past treaty did not sufficiently resolve the issue because it was framed as a universal violation of human rights, and the other party believes that the issue has been resolved by the past treaty because it was framed as a diplomatic issue, then this difference in frames will make it difficult for the two parties to reach a compromise. Is it possible for Japan and Korea to share the same perspective on the comfort women issue? The Korean news framing and the Asahi's news framing are similar in that they both adopt a human rights frame and a war responsibility frame. However, in Japan, the framing of the comfort women issue is buried in the ideological conflict of conservative versus liberal, making it difficult for Asahi's framing to be shared beyond the ideological cleavage. In addition, although the framing of the issue as one of the contentious issues in East Asian diplomacy, as currently adopted by Yomiuri, is not prominent in Korea, there may be a possibility of sharing frames with conservative newspapers in Korea in more pragmatic diplomatic frames. For example, if Japan and Korea share the perspective that diplomatic and security cooperation between the two countries is necessary to counter the threat of North Korea, there is a possibility that conservative newspapers in Japan and Korea could partially share the diplomatic frame. If this happens, it may be possible for the liberal newspapers, Asahi and Hankyoreh, and the conservative newspapers, Yomiuri and Chosun Ilbo, to share their respective perspectives.

However, given the current consistency of news frames in Korean newspapers, it will be difficult in the short term to resolve the differences in frames between the two countries. While news frames affect public opinion, audience attitudes affect the tone of the newspaper. As long as the Korean public perceives the comfort women issue using a frame similar to the newspaper reporting frame, it is difficult for the newspapers to adopt a frame that deviates significantly from it. For example, it would be difficult for Chosun Ilbo to trivialize and frame the comfort women issue as one of the resolved diplomatic issues just because it is conservative. In particular, there is a dominant critical public opinion in Korea against those people and companies that are considered to have been friendly to Japan's colonial rule in the past. Under these circumstances, it would be difficult for Korean newspapers to adopt the same frame of reference used by conservative newspapers in Japan. Thus, the difference in reporting frames between Japan and Korea revealed in this study is considered to be one of the factors that make the resolution of the comfort women issue difficult.

Note

1 We would like to express our gratitude to Prof. Kyu S. Hahn and Ms. Seulgi Jang of Seoul National University for collecting and providing the Korean newspaper data.

References

Iyengar, S. (1991). *Is anyone responsible? How television frames political issues.* Chicago, IL: University of Chicago Press.

Lee, G. (2007). A content analysis of Korean TV news coverage on Japan. *Keio Media Communications Research, 57*, 35–48. (In Japanese)

Lee, Y.-M., & Min, Y. (2011). Social movements and media frame: Collective action frames of the Japanese "comfort women" issue. *Media, Gender & Culture, 19*, 39–70. (In Korean)

Lee, W. S., Bae, J. Y., & Park, K. W. (2016). Korean media's news coverage of Japan's position on her past history problems under Abe Shinzo's cabinet: Dynamic process of news framing. *Korean Journal of Communication and Information, 79*, 104–139. (In Korean)

Mikolov, T., Sutskever, I., Chen, K., Corrado, G., & Dean, J. (2013). Distributed representations of words and phrases and their compositionality. *In Proceedings of NIPS, 2013*. Neural Information Processing Systems Foundation. Retrieved from http://arxiv.org/pdf/1310.4546.pdf

Moon, S. J., & Sung, J. Y. (2006). Exposure to negative media issue and anti-Japanese sentiment. *Korean Journal of Broadcasting and Telecommunication Studies, 20*(5), 70–105. (In Korean)

Oh, D. Y. (2011). Frame difference analysis on the news of Korean and Japanese newspapers regarding the 100th anniversary of Japan's colonization of Korea. *Korean Journal of Journalism and Communication Studies, 55*(1), 140–168. (In Korean)

Pak, H. J. (2016). News reporting on comfort women: Framing, frame difference, and frame changing in four South Korean and Japanese newspapers, 1998–2013. *Journalism & Mass Communication Quarterly, 93*(4), 1006–1025.

Park, Y. H., & Chung, J. H. (2020). How did the press report the conflict between Korea and Japan? Focusing on framing and signifying strategies. *Journal of the Korea Contents Association, 20*(7), 352–367. (In Korean)

Semetko, H. A., & Valkenburg, P. M. (2000). Framing European politics: A content analysis of press and television news. *Journal of Communication, 50*(2), 93–109.

Takekawa, S. (2016). Reconciliation prospects and divided war memories in Japan: An analysis of major newspapers on the comfort women issue. In M. Kim (Ed.) *Routledge Handbook of Memory and Reconciliation in East Asia* (pp. 79–94). New York and London: Routledge Taylor & Francis Group.

Yang, J. (2003). Framing the NATO air strikes on Kosovo across countries: Comparison of Chinese and US newspaper coverage. *Gazette, 65*(3), 231–249.

7 The influence of anti-Korean sentiment on communications with political parties

Mitsuo Yoshida, Fujio Toriumi

A partial amendment of Japan's Public Officers Election Act in 2013 lifted the ban on election campaigning via the Internet. Since then, the use of social media platforms such as Twitter and Facebook during elections has become essential for political parties seeking to disseminate information to supporters and attract new supporters. However, there are also reports that the impact of the Internet on elections is limited, so it is not yet clear what uses of the Internet are effective election strategies in Japan.

In Internet campaigning, political parties propagate their messages extensively on social media. Unlike conventional media such as newspapers and TV, social media allow push-type information diffusion; information is conveyed by spreading behavior, such as the retweeting of other users' tweets even to those who are initially uninterested in political information. Therefore, political parties expect their official account content to spread on social media through retweets and the parties' information to be disseminated to the broader public.

Political parties also play an important role in public opinion on diplomacy and international relations. Political parties attempt to win voter support by catering to their preferences and/or persuading them with policy packages, including those on foreign affairs. When negative feelings toward a foreign country are strong, parties and politicians may try to capitalize on such feelings to strengthen their support base. This chapter focuses on the relationship between anti-Korean sentiment and party communications on Twitter in Japan, and examines how communication emanating from political parties diffuses in different ways depending on the existence or nonexistence of anti-Korean sentiment among those who retweet such messages. For example, are users who express anti-Korean sentiment more likely to retweet tweets from conservative parties?

As mentioned above, in modern national elections, political parties use social media to promote policies and candidates by communicating with voters. Although US-centered studies of presidential elections have shown

DOI: 10.4324/9781003143536-7

fragmentation between the two parties' supporters, the level of fragmentation among social media users in a multi-party country such as Japan remains unclear. In 2017, in South Korea (hereafter, Korea), President Park was replaced by President Moon Jae-in, who changed the country's policy toward Japan. Then, in September 2017, a statue commemorating so-called comfort women was designated a public artifact by Jongno District in Seoul, increasing some Japanese voters' negative sentiment toward Korea. To determine how this dislike of other countries affects communications with political parties in the home country, we focused on anti-Korean sentiment, which is increasingly a wedge factor in Japanese public opinion. This chapter analyzes the state of communication between political parties and voters on Twitter, focusing on the 48th House of Representatives election in Japan in 2017. Specifically, it examines two types of communication between political parties and Twitter users: 1) users' exposure to tweets by political parties, and 2) retweeting party tweets. In this analysis, we focus on the effects on users who express anti-Korean sentiment, hereinafter called "anti-Korean users."

In analyzing this communication, we focus on the number of users to whom each party's information (in the form of tweets) was delivered. In other words, one of our aims is to obtain accurate information regarding the diffusion power for each party rather than just the number of followers. To this end, we address the following five research questions:

[RQ1] Political interest of anti-Korean users: Is the existence or non-existence of anti-Korean sentiment related to political interest?

[RQ2] Partisanship of anti-Korean users: Is there a difference in the ratio of retweeters and followers with anti-Korean sentiment across political parties?

[RQ3] Redundancy of political parties' followers: Who is following the followers of political party accounts? What are their characteristics when this is narrowed down to anti-Korean users?

[RQ4] Activeness of political parties' followers: How many retweets were by followers of a party account? Did anti-Korean users retweet more actively than others?

[RQ5] Power of political parties to spread their messages: How many tweets were delivered to nonpartisan users? What roles do anti-Korean users play in the delivery of political party information to users?

Related work

An increasing number of studies have examined users' access to political information on social media (Gayo-Avello, 2013; Jungherr, 2016; Tucker et al., 2018). As an illustration, Tumasjan et al. (2010) reported that Twitter functions as a discussion forum for politics, finding that the mere number of Twitter mentions of a party resembles its election result. Adamic and Glance (2005) studied the linking patterns and discussion topics of political blogs, finding differences in the behavior of liberal and conservative blogs, with conservative blogs linking to each other more tightly. Such studies typically target the propagation of and exposure to news on social media (Hayat & Samuel-Azran, 2017; Hyun & Moon, 2014; Iyengar & Hahn, 2009). In other words, previous studies have not explicitly examined tweets posted by political parties and those who retweet them but merely analyzed the linkages and the number of messages/followers. Previous studies also show ideological fragmentation on social media (Barberá et al., 2015; Batorski & Grzywińska, 2018; Dahlgren, 2005; Williams et al., 2015). These studies were interested in supporters of specific political parties and focused on those who received political information directly from parties. However, there are known to be many nonpartisan voters in Japan. Therefore, when analyzing social media, it is also necessary to focus on nonpartisan users who receive political information indirectly through other users.

In addition, many of the previous studies on the propagation of information on social media have focused on the number of followers as a measure of social influence. However, the number of followers does not necessarily indicate the power to disseminate information, especially when followers can be purchased and their numbers padded (Bakshy et al., 2011; Cha et al., 2010; Cresci et al., 2015; Stringhini et al., 2013). Therefore, the power of information diffusion cannot be measured by the mere number of followers. This study analyzes the diffusion of party tweets in more detail by focusing not on the number of followers but on the information diffusion behavior: i.e., retweeting. In doing so, we focus on the level of anti-Korean sentiment as a key user characteristic. In Japan in recent years, online hate speech against Koreans and the Korean minority living in Japan has emerged to become a major social issue (Itagaki, 2015; Ito, 2014; Yamaguchi, 2013). In addition, there have been cases of conservative politicians disseminating factually inaccurate negative information about Korean minorities on social media. So, there is a growing need to analyze the relationship between political parties and politicians, and voter sentiment toward Korea. This study aims to clarify how the diffusion of information by political parties on Twitter is related to users' anti-Korean sentiment.

The analyses in this chapter are based on two previously published studies (Yoshida & Toriumi, 2018a, 2018b), but we reanalyzed our raw Twitter data to answer specific questions related to anti-Korean sentiment. Therefore, some results (especially the number of tweets and users) may differ from the published results. Below, we present all the data and indicators used in the subsequent analysis, followed by the results.

Dataset

In this study, we used retweets in the Japanese language collected from Twitter in 2017. The data were collected using the Twitter search API[1] and amounted to 4,552,510,103 retweets (from 32,389,758 users). These were retweets of 522,036,378 original tweets (from 16,175,488 users). Normally, tweets collected using the Twitter streaming API and the "follow" parameter are used in studies focusing on specific users. However, because we started this study after this election had finished, we decided to extract the necessary data from the collected retweets.

First, we used all the data from 2017 to extract tweets from all users expressing anti-Korean sentiment. Specifically, we extracted tweets that include the terms "在日" (Zainichi: resident in Japan),[2] "韓国人" (South Korean), "朝鮮人" (Korean), and "チョン" (Chon: pejorative term for Koreans). These words were selected following Taka's (2015) classification, which identified common derogatory terms for Koreans. However, as the following analyses do not manually screen the tweets owing to the massive volume of data, the possibility of some positive references being included cannot be completely ruled out (e.g., "Korean" to indicate K-pop stars). In this study, for comprehensive analysis, we use tweets from all the identified users without filters such as a minimum number of tweets. The above words were tweeted by 146,076 users, or 0.9% of users whose words were retweeted in 2017. These anti-Korean tweets were retweeted by 965,435 users (3.0%), indicating that anti-Korean tweets tend to be retweeted more often than others.

Next, we extracted the Twitter retweets from September 28 to October 23, 2017. This period encompasses the 48th general election for the Lower House in Japan. Japan's Public Officers Election Act severely limits the period during which campaign documents can be distributed. This regulation applies to both candidates and voters, and election-related tweets are regarded as campaign documents. A total of 382,119,922 retweets were identified during this period. To focus only on data related to politics, we targeted the official accounts of political parties and selected the accounts of the six major parties. These political parties are shown in Table 7.1. The Liberal Democratic Party of Japan (LDP) and Komeito are the ruling parties, and the LDP is known as a conservative party. The Constitutional Democratic Party of Japan (CDP) is known as a liberal party. The CDP and the Party of Hope (Kibounotou) are new political parties formed shortly before this election. We only use 770,064 retweets (collected from

Table 7.1 Major political parties in Japan

Political party name	Account name	Tweets	Retweeted	Followers	Seats
Liberal Democratic Party of Japan (LDP)	@jimin_koho	300	12,0391	134,590	284
Constitutional Democratic Party of Japan (CDP)	@CDP2017	929	527,091	190,965	55
Party of Hope (Kibounotou)	@kibounotou	429	22,516	13,528	50
Komeito	@komei_koho	305	31,919	76,742	29
Japanese Communist Party (JCP)	@jcp_cc	350	54,528	42,507	12
Japan Innovation Party (JIP)	@osaka_ishin	294	13,618	15,953	11

86,136 users) of tweets from these political parties. A total of 86,136 users retweeted party tweets during the election, of which 14,579 (16.9%) were from users who expressed anti-Korean sentiment.

Figures 7.1 and 7.2 show the number of tweets from six political parties and the number of times these were retweeted. Under Japanese law, political parties cannot call for votes during the actual voting time (7 am to 8 pm on October 22, 2017), which is why the number of tweets on election day was relatively low. The number of tweets by the Japanese Communist Party (JCP) increased on the eve of the election, and the number of tweets by the LDP increased on the day. The JCP called for votes the day before the election, and the LDP reported each time its candidates had secured election. It seems that the number of retweets was greatly affected by the number of followers. As shown in Table 7.1, the CDP has many followers, so its tweets were frequently retweeted.

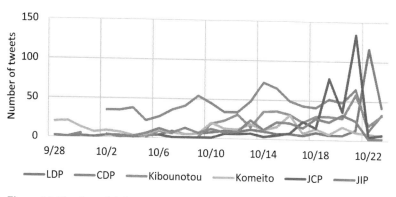

Figure 7.1 Number of daily tweets by political parties.

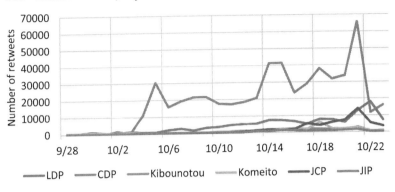

Figure 7.2 Number of retweets of political party tweets.

Next, we used tweets from the 86,136 users who retweeted political party tweets, gathering their tweets from April 10, 2007 to November 14, 2017. In this way, we collected and used 197,267,467 tweets, including retweets.[3] These data were used to estimate the level of political interest of 86,136 users, which was measured by the number of political tweets. We used machine learning to determine whether each tweet was political. First, we manually classified a random sample of 9,500 original tweets into political or general (i.e., nonpolitical) tweets.[4] Then, the system used these as training data to learn to classify tweets using a support vector machine (SVM), logistic regression, and convolutional neural networks (CNN). In SVM and logistic regression, the tweets were converted into a bag-of-words normalized by term frequency–inverse document frequency (TF–IDF) and learned. In CNN, words used in tweets were converted into word distribution expressions obtained by fastText and learned. The performance was verified using 70% of the entire corpus as learning data and 30% as test data for the three methods. The accuracies for SVM, logistic regression, and CNN were 0.671, 0.727, and 0.839, respectively. From this, we confirmed that CNN could extract political tweets with the highest accuracy. This result shows the same trend reported by Oliveira et al. (2018), who classified Brazilian tweets into political and general tweets.

To identify the people exposed to party tweets, we used a social graph of Twitter users. First, we gathered followers of the major parties. Then, we created a combined set of these users and those who retweeted tweets from the major parties. This set includes 416,451 users who follow a political party or retweet its tweets. Finally, we identified their followers as of November 10, 2017, and built the social graph, which consists of 57,987,463 nodes (users) and 228,037,571 edges (followee–follower links). Figure 7.3 provides an overview of this graph. "OAs" are political

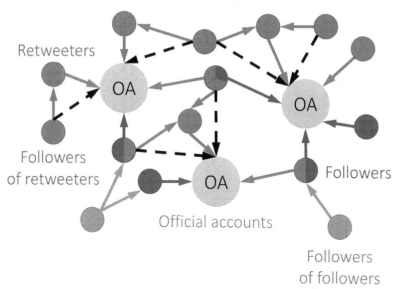

Figure 7.3 Overview of the social graph.

parties' official accounts. The orange nodes represent 86,136 retweeters. There are 381,800 followers of OAs represented by the blue nodes. The unique combination of orange and blue is 416,451 users. These 416,451 users received party tweets directly during the election, and 22,112 (5.3%) of these users expressed anti-Korean sentiment. The ratio of 5.3% is high, given that only 0.9% expressed anti-Korean sentiment throughout 2017. In addition, although only 20.7% (86,136/416,451) of users actively disseminate (retweet) information about political parties during the election, the proportion is as high as 65.9% (14,579/22,112) if limited to anti-Korean users. It is strongly suggested that anti-Korean users tend to retweet political party messages more than others.

To quantify the parties' ability to disseminate their messages, we focus on nonpartisan users. We define nonpartisan users according to the following criteria: those who indirectly received party tweets via retweets AND those who neither followed any party nor retweeted any of their tweets. They are represented as the green nodes in Figure 7.3, and the dashed line represents the indirect reception of party tweets through retweets. There were 16,417,084 nonpartisan users, or 97.6% of the 16,823,989 users (including orange, blue, and green nodes), who received party tweets either directly or indirectly. It is vital for political parties to deliver their messages to nonpartisan users because there are many of them. Of the anti-Korean users, 81,506 (55.8%) received party tweets directly or indirectly. The proportion of nonpartisan users who did not receive political information directly was 97.6% overall, while that of anti-Korean users was 73.3%. That is, anti-Korean users are more likely to receive political information directly from political parties than other users.

Results and discussion

Political interest of anti-Korean users

When negative feelings toward a foreign country are strong, parties and politicians may try to capitalize on such feelings to strengthen their support base. Therefore, it is hypothesized that users with negative feelings about a foreign country have a strong interest in politics. Because this chapter focuses on users who express anti-Korean sentiment, we investigated their level of political interest.

As described in the Dataset section, we examined all 197,267,467 tweets obtained from the timeline of retweeters (86,136 users). An estimated 11,635,182 of these tweets (5.9%) were political. These were tweeted by 69,117 users, of whom 12,495 (18.1%) expressed anti-Korean sentiment. Figure 7.4 shows the number of political tweets from each user; those who posted no political tweets are omitted. Figure 7.4 shows that anti-Korean users tend to tweet about politics more frequently than others.

To estimate whether a tweet is a political tweet using the CNN method, its level of "politicalness" is calculated. This level takes a value from 0 to 1, and those tweets exceeding 0.5 are considered to be political. The closer this value is to 1, the more political is the content of the tweet. Figure 7.5 shows the distribution of the average politicalness of the tweets by each user. Here,

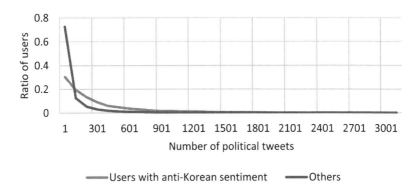

Figure 7.4 Number of political tweets by users with and without anti-Korean sentiment.

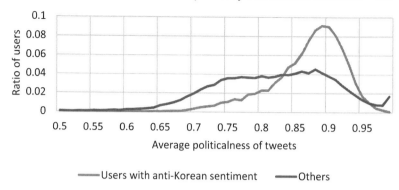

Figure 7.5 Average politicalness of tweets by users with and without anti-Korean sentiment.

the politicalness of each tweet is averaged and plotted for each user. This shows that users with anti-Korean sentiment not only post many political tweets, but their tweets tend to have more explicitly political content.

Partisanship of anti-Korean users

How much did each party rely on the power of users who expressed anti-Korean sentiment? In this section, we focus on retweeters and followers who spread party tweets.

Table 7.2 shows the number of users (retweeters) who retweeted tweets from each political party and the number of anti-Korean users among them. Retweeters can generally be considered those who have an affinity

Table 7.2 Number of users (retweeters) who retweet tweets from each political party

Political party name	Account name	Retweeters	Proportion of anti-Korean users
Liberal Democratic Party of Japan (LDP)	@jimin_koho	22,102	7,296 (33.0%)
Constitutional Democratic Party of Japan (CDP)	@CDP2017	51,857	6,681 (12.9%)
Party of Hope (Kibounotou)	@kibounotou	3,736	722 (19.3%)
Komeito	@komei_koho	10,239	1,549 (15.1%)
Japanese Communist Party (JCP)	@jcp_cc	11,685	2,535 (21.7%)
Japan Innovation Party (JIP)	@osaka_ishin	1,851	606 (32.7%)

with a political party because they can deliver party information to users who do not follow it. As shown in Table 7.2, the ratios of anti-Korean retweeters vary greatly across parties. The LDP and the Japan Innovation Party (JIP) have a high ratio of anti-Korean users. These parties are known to be conservative parties in Japan. On the other hand, the ratio is low for the CDP, the largest liberal party in Japan. Somewhat unexpectedly, the JCP, also known as the liberal party, has a relatively high ratio of such users. When we probe into the overlap of anti-Korean users between LDP and JCP retweeters, only 252 of JCP retweeters were also LDP retweeters. Similarly, the overlap between LDP and CDP was only 695 retweeters. These results show that anti-Korean users who spread tweets from conservative parties differ from anti-Korean users who spread the tweets of liberal parties, suggesting different motivations.

Table 7.3 shows the number of followers of each political party and the number of anti-Korean users among them. Followers are passive supporters who are constantly informed of political parties and can be thought of as reserve forces for dissemination (retweeting). Because there are more followers than retweeters, the proportion of anti-Korean users is relatively low. Among the conservative parties, the ratio of the JIP is still high, but that of the LDP is somewhat lower. Because the ratio of anti-Korean users to retweeters and that of anti-Korean users to followers are not necessarily consistent, it is difficult to discuss the characteristics of followers of a certain political party based solely on the proportion of anti-Korean users.

To analyze the characteristics of anti-Korean users (both retweeters and followers) demonstrated by members of each political party, we

Table 7.3 Number of political party twitter followers

Political party name	Account name	Followers	Proportion of anti-Korean users
Liberal Democratic Party of Japan (LDP)	@jimin_koho	134,590	8,146 (6.1%)
Constitutional Democratic Party of Japan (CDP)	@CDP2017	190,965	7,998 (4.2%)
Party of Hope (Kibounotou)	@kibounotou	13,528	870 (6.4%)
Komeito	@komei_koho	76,742	1,512 (2.0%)
Japanese Communist Party (JCP)	@jcp_cc	42,507	3,026 (7.1%)
Japan Innovation Party (JIP)	@osaka_ishin	15,953	1,945 (12.2%)

investigated the hashtags used. The tweets used in the investigation contain derogatory terms for Koreans in 2017, as described in the Dataset section. Anti-Korean users who follow the LDP used hashtags that certainly made them appear anti-Korean, such as "朝鮮人," "在日," and "反日" (anti-Japanese). On the other hand, anti-Korean users who follow the CDP and JCP also used many hashtags that seemed to have nothing to do with anti-Korean sentiment, such as "ユチョン" (Park Yoo-chun: Korean singer/songwriter)[5] and "ヤバすぎる緊急事態条項" (Danger of emergency clause). These results suggest that CDP and JCP users may include a significant number of pro-Korean users.

Redundancy of political parties' followers

Redundancy of followers is measured by the extent of overlap between followers of a political party and their followers. Political parties can deliver messages to their followers, but they cannot directly deliver them to non-followers. If followers retweet party tweets, the messages spread beyond the parties' immediate followers. If all followers of party followers also follow the party (i.e., if the redundancy is high), even if the party's followers retweet the party's tweets, the information is delivered only to its own followers. The smaller the overlap between the immediate followers of a party account and its followers is, the lower is the redundancy and the greater is its ability to spread information.

Figure 7.6 shows the redundancy of followers of each political party. The x-axis indicates the level of redundancy. For example, if user X, who follows party Y, has ten followers and six of them follow party Y, then the x-axis indicates 0.6. The y-axis indicates the cumulative share of such users among the followers of a political party. As an illustration, for 63.7% of

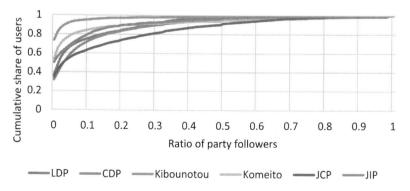

Figure 7.6 Redundancy of followers (redundancy is lower at the upper left and higher at the lower right).

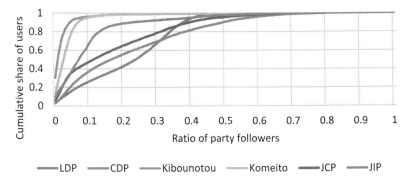

Figure 7.7 Redundancy of anti-Korean followers.

JCP followers, 10% or fewer of their followers follow the JCP (x-axis = 0.1 and y-axis = 0.637). In other words, for 36.3% of JCP followers, more than 10% of their followers also follow the JCP, indicating a high redundancy of JCP followers. Note that high redundancy means that the community of supporters (followers) develops and its social graph is dense. If we compare the two political parties formed roughly at the same time, one new party—the CDP—succeeded in creating a community, but the other, Kibounotou, failed. Among the followers of Kibounotou, 73.5% were users whose followers did not follow Kibounotou. In contrast, the JCP was most successful in creating a cohesive community. Figure 7.7 shows the results of the same analysis as in Figure 7.6, but only for anti-Korean users. The curve of the graph in Figure 7.7 is on the lower right-hand side compared with Figure 7.6. This change is especially remarkable for the LDP. That is, anti-Korean users are creating a cohesive community among followers of the LDP.

A highly cohesive group of followers tends not to follow other political parties. Figure 7.8 shows the rate of duplicate followers for each party. For

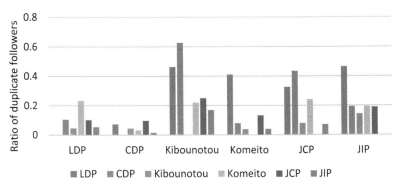

Figure 7.8 Duplication of followers.

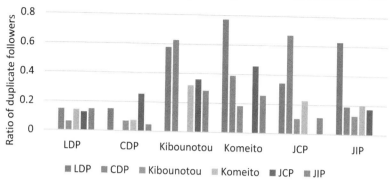

Figure 7.9 Duplication of followers with anti-Korean sentiment.

example, about 63% of the followers of Kibounotou also follow the CDP. The CDP followers typically do not follow other parties. Such users only receive information from a specific party. Therefore, the parties can deliver their information to such users intensively. Followers of parties with low redundancy (i.e., Kibounotou) tend to follow other political parties as well. Figure 7.9 shows the same results as in Figure 7.8 but only for anti-Korean users. It can be seen that such users tend to follow various political parties, compared with the overall pattern illustrated in Figure 7.8. In fact, aside from the proportion of LDP followers following the Komeito, all the proportions are higher in Figure 7.9 than in Figure 7.8. The reason for this is presumably that anti-Korean users tend to be more interested in politics, as shown in Figures 7.4 and 7.5.

Duplication of retweeters is different from duplication of followers. Figure 7.10 shows the rate of duplicate retweeters for each political party.

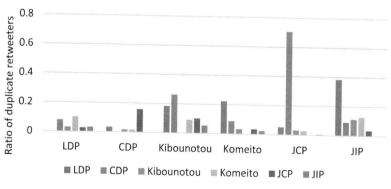

Figure 7.10 Duplication of retweeters.

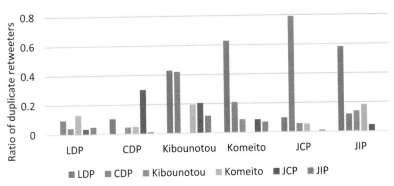

Figure 7.11 Duplication of retweeters with anti-Korean sentiment.

For example, about 70% of the retweeters of the JCP also retweet CDP tweets. The retweeters of the LDP typically do not follow other political parties. Such users only spread tweets from the parties they support but do not help others. Therefore, political parties are strongly encouraged by such users to spread their tweets. Figure 7.11 shows the same results as in Figure 7.10 but only for anti-Korean users. It can be seen that these users tend to retweet more of various parties' tweets than those illustrated in Figure 7.10. In particular, retweeters from each party are more likely to retweet LDP tweets.

Activeness of political parties' followers

The activeness of party followers is measured by the ratio of party followers who retweet tweets from the party. For political parties to deliver information to the broader public, their followers are expected to retweet party messages frequently because most users are nonpartisan and do not follow the parties' accounts. If none of a political party's followers retweet, the party can deliver information only to its immediate followers. Even if tweets are delivered to users via retweets, users do not necessarily see them. In this analysis, we focus on whether political parties can deliver information to the wider public. So, we do not consider whether users actually read the tweets.

Figure 7.12 shows the activeness of the followers of each party. For example, 18.5% of CDP followers retweeted at least one tweet from the CDP. This is higher than the figure for other parties. The CDP was founded recently, on October 2, 2017, and followers are limited to Twitter users at that time. In general, older users who created their accounts a long time ago tend to be inactive. Such users do not read tweets or retweet, even if

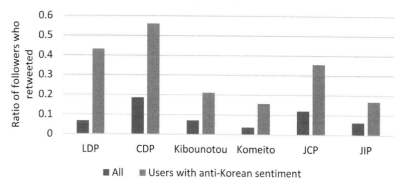

Figure 7.12 Ratio of retweeters to followers.

they follow a political party. Therefore, followers of older party accounts are less active, while followers of newer parties are more active. However, even though Kibounotou is also a new party, the activeness of its followers is low. Kibounotou retweeters tend not to follow the party, as shown in Figure 7.13. That is, Kibounotou has failed to acquire active followers but has succeeded in acquiring non-follower retweeters. The redundancy of Kibounotou followers is low (Figures 7.6 and 7.7), so Kibounotou can deliver information to a variety of users and as a result, non-followers may retweet frequently.

As shown in Figure 7.12, anti-Korean users are more likely than others to retweet tweets from the political parties they follow. This tendency appears for all political parties. Presumably, anti-Korean users have more interest in politics, as shown in Figures 7.4 and 7.5. As mentioned above, although both the LDP and CDP have active followers who express anti-Korean sentiment, their motivations for retweeting may be different.

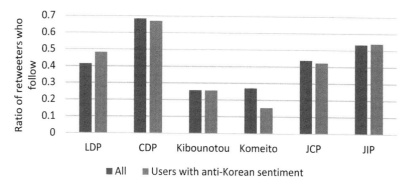

Figure 7.13 Ratio of party followers to retweeters.

On the other hand, as shown in Figure 7.13, aside from Komeito, the proportion of followers among retweeters was largely unaffected by anti-Korean sentiment. Komeito retweeters are less likely to follow Komeito, and this tendency is even stronger among anti-Korean retweeters.

Power of political parties to spread their messages

The power of political parties to spread their messages is measured by the number of users who received their tweets. The number of times a user received tweets from a party is calculated as follows. If the user is a follower of the political party, the number of the tweets of political parties is used; otherwise, the number of times that the followees of the user (i.e., the accounts that the user follows) retweeted the party tweets. We assume that a user "received" the tweets from a political party when they appear on the user's timeline. So, we do not consider whether users actually read them. In this section, we analyze how many party tweets were received during the election period.

Figure 7.14 indicates the political parties' power to spread tweets by showing the average number of recipients. As explained in the Data section, nonpartisan users are those who receive tweets indirectly via retweets. These users are assumed to have relatively low interest in politics, and political parties need to communicate with these users proactively. The CDP was only the second most powerful, despite having the most followers. This is because it has high redundancy among its followers, as demonstrated above. When users are highly redundant and their communities are highly cohesive, messages from political parties are less likely

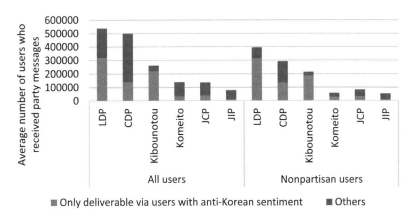

Figure 7.14 Political parties' power to spread messages. The orange bar shows the number of tweets that could only be delivered via anti-Korean users.

to spread beyond the community, resulting in limited information propagation. That is, the power to spread information cannot be measured by the number of followers alone. The LDP has solid power to spread its messages, while that of Komeito is weak, although both are ruling parties.

How do anti-Korean users influence political parties' power to spread messages? The orange bars in Figure 7.14 show the number of users who could only receive party tweets through anti-Korean users. In other words, political parties can deliver tweets only to users designated as "Others," if the anti-Korean users were removed from the social graph. As shown in Figure 7.14, anti-Korean users contribute significantly to spreading LDP and Kibounotou tweets. If there were no anti-Korean users, the LDP would be unable to deliver more tweets than the CDP, suggesting that the LDP is heavily dependent on anti-Korean users to spread their messages to the public. More specifically, 59.2% of users who received the LDP tweets would not have done so without retweets by anti-Korean users, which is far higher than the ratio of anti-Korean retweeters among LDP followers (33.0%, see Table 7.2). These results indicate that a small number of anti-Korean LDP followers strongly influence the spread of party messages. In contrast, liberal parties such as the CDP and JCP deliver tweets to users without relying greatly on anti-Korean users.

Conclusion

Focusing on users who express anti-Korean sentiment, we analyzed the social graphs and retweeters of tweets from political parties during the 48th general election for Japan's Lower House in 2017. This study was intended to elucidate the political parties' power to disseminate their messages on Twitter, with a specific focus on the roles played by anti-Korean users during the propagation process.

The results indicate that anti-Korean users had a stronger political interest than other users, and they tended to retweet conservative parties' tweets. The ratio of anti-Korean users to party retweeters was highest for the LDP (33.0%). If we focus on the followers of each political party, users following JCP followers also tended to follow the JCP, indicating high redundancy among JCP followers. The redundancy is even higher if the focus is limited to users who express anti-Korean sentiment. This increase was particularly remarkable among LDP followers. We also found that followers of the liberal CDP frequently retweeted CDP tweets. However, because the redundancy of CDP followers is high, the CDP was unable to reach any more users than the LDP despite having more followers and retweeters. The most important finding of this study is that a small number of anti-Korean users play a crucial role in spreading conservative parties' messages, particularly those from the LDP.

Although the CDP appears to have more power to disseminate tweets than the LDP when only the number of followers is considered, this study shows that the LDP actually delivers its messages to more users. The gap in spreading power between the LDP and CDP is even larger when we limit our focus to reaching nonpartisan users who receive political party messages indirectly. The strong spreading power of the LDP is achieved by users with the anti-Korean sentiment. In 2017, anti-Korean users accounted for only 0.9% of all users but 33.0% of LDP retweeters, and they delivered LDP tweets to 59.2% of all recipients of LDP messages. When it comes to LDP tweets reaching nonpartisan users, 79.4% of nonpartisan users received LDP tweets via anti-Korean users. In other words, the LDP relies heavily on such users to disseminate its messages to users, especially nonpartisan users. In contrast, only 12.9% of CDP retweeters expressed anti-Korean sentiment, and they delivered CDP tweets to 28.0% of all recipients. In the 48th general election for the Lower House in Japan, anti-Korean users, as strong supporters of the conservative party, helped to spread its tweets.

Notes

1 We conducted all searches using the "RT lang:ja" query.
2 The original meaning of "Zainichi" is "in Japan," but for historical reasons, it is often used as an abbreviation for "Korean residents in Japan." Moreover, when used in such a sense, it often has a discriminatory connotation.
3 Owing to the limitations of the Twitter API, it is limited to a maximum of 3,200 tweets per user.
4 This classification work and estimation by machine learning described later use the results of Yoshida and Toriumi (2018b).
5 "チョン" is a substring of "ユチョン." We attempted to extract anti-Korean tweets using "チョン" but in so doing, we also extracted tweets that are considered to be pro-Korean, including "ユチョン." Most users who posted tweets containing the "ユチョン" hashtag were CDP followers.

References

Adamic, L. A., & Glance, N. (2005). The political blogosphere and the 2004 US election: Divided they blog. *LinkKDD '05: Proceedings of the 3rd international workshop on link discovery* (pp. 36–43). https://doi.org/10.1145/1134271.1134277
Bakshy, E., Hofman, J. M., Mason, W. A., & Watts, D. J. (2011). Everyone's an influencer: Quantifying influence on Twitter. *WSDM '11: Proceedings of the fourth ACM international conference on web search and data mining* (pp. 65–74). https://doi.org/10.1145/1935826.1935845
Barberá, P., Jost, J. T., Nagler, J. Tucker, J. A., & Bonneau, R. (2015). Tweeting from left to right: Is online political communication more than an echo chamber? *Psychological Science*, *26*(10), 1531–1542. https://doi.org/10.1177%2F0956797615594620

Batorski, D., & Grzywińska, I. (2018). Three dimensions of the public sphere on Facebook. *Information, Communication & Society, 21*(3), 356–374. https://doi.org/10.1080/1369118X.2017.1281329

Cha, M., Haddadi, H., Benevenuto, F., & Gummadi, K. P. (2010). Measuring user influence in Twitter: The million follower fallacy. *Proceedings of the fourth international AAAI conference on weblogs and social media* (pp. 10–17). https://www.aaai.org/ocs/index.php/ICWSM/ICWSM10/paper/view/1538

Cresci, S., Di Pietro, R., Petrocchi, M., Spognardi, A., & Tesconi, M. (2015). Fame for sale: Efficient detection of fake Twitter followers. *Decision Support Systems, 80*, 56–71. https://doi.org/10.1016/j.dss.2015.09.003

Dahlgren, P. (2005). The Internet, public spheres, and political communication: Dispersion and deliberation. *Political Communication, 22*(2), 147–162. https://doi.org/10.1080/10584600590933160

Gayo-Avello, D. (2013). A meta-analysis of state-of-the-art electoral prediction from Twitter data. *Social Science Computer Review, 31*(6), 649–679. https://doi.org/10.1177%2F0894439313493979

Hayat, T., & Samuel-Azran, T. (2017). "You too, second screeners?" Second screeners' echo chambers during the 2016 US elections primaries. *Journal of Broadcasting & Electronic Media, 61*(2), 291–308. https://doi.org/10.1080/08838151.2017.1309417

Hyun, K. D., & Moon, S. J. (2014). News media's role in the issue-voting process: News attention, issue proximity, and vote choice. *Journalism & Mass Communication Quarterly, 91*(4), 687–705. https://doi.org/10.1177%2F1077699014550095

Itagaki, R. (2015). The anatomy of Korea-phobia in Japan. *Japanese Studies, 35*(1), 49–66. https://doi.org/10.1080/10371397.2015.1007496

Ito, K. (2014). Anti-Korean sentiment and hate speech in the current Japan: A report from the street. *Procedia Environmental Sciences, 20*, 434–443. https://doi.org/10.1016/j.proenv.2014.03.055

Iyengar, S., & Hahn, K. S. (2009). Red media, blue media: Evidence of ideological selectivity in media use. *Journal of Communication, 59*(1), 19–39. https://doi.org/10.1111/j.1460-2466.2008.01402.x

Jungherr, A. (2016). Twitter use in election campaigns: A systematic literature review. *Journal of Information Technology & Politics, 13*(1), 72–91. https://doi.org/10.1080/19331681.2015.1132401

Oliveira, L. S., Vaz de Melo, P. O. S., Amaral, M. S., & Pinho, J. A. G. (2018). When politicians talk about politics: Identifying political tweets of Brazilian congressmen. *Proceedings of the twelfth international AAAI conference on web and social media* (pp. 664–667). https://www.aaai.org/ocs/index.php/ICWSM/ICWSM18/paper/view/17824

Stringhini, G., Wang, G., Egele, M., Kruegel, C., Vigna, G., Zheng, H., & Zhao, B. Y. (2013). Follow the green: Growth and dynamics in Twitter follower markets. In *IMC '13: Proceedings of the 2013 Internet measurement conference* (pp. 163–176). https://doi.org/10.1145/2504730.2504731

Taka, F. (2015). *The anatomy of racism: Prejudice against Zainichi Koreans in the age of the Internet*. Keiso Shobo. [in Japanese]

Tucker, J., Guess, A., Barbera, P., Vaccari, C., Siegel, A., Sanovich, S., Stukal, D., & Nyhan, B. (2018). Social media, political polarization, and political disinformation: A review of the scientific literature. *SSRN Electronic Journal*. https://dx.doi.org/10.2139/ssrn.3144139

Tumasjan, A., Sprenger, T., Sandner, P., & Welpe, I. (2010). Predicting elections with Twitter: What 140 characters reveal about political sentiment. *Proceedings of the fourth international AAAI conference on weblogs and social media* (pp. 178–185). https://www.aaai.org/ocs/index.php/ICWSM/ICWSM10/paper/view/1441

Williams, H. T. P., McMurray, J. R., Kurz, T., & Lambert, F. H. (2015). Network analysis reveals open forums and echo chambers in social media discussions of climate change. *Global Environmental Change*, *32*, 126–138. https://doi.org/10.1016/j.gloenvcha.2015.03.006

Yamaguchi, T. (2013). Xenophobia in action: Ultranationalism, hate speech, and the Internet in Japan. *Radical History Review*, *2013*(117), 98–118. https://doi.org/10.1215/01636545-2210617

Yoshida, M., & Toriumi, F. (2018a). Information diffusion power of political party Twitter accounts during Japan's 2017 election. In: S. Staab, O. Koltsova, & D. Ignatov (Eds.), *Social informatics. SocInfo 2018. Lecture Notes in Computer Science* (vol. 11186, pp. 334–342). Springer. https://doi.org/10.1007/978-3-030-01159-8_32

Yoshida, M., & Toriumi, F. (2018b). Analysis of political party Twitter accounts' retweeters during Japan's 2017 election. *Proceedings of the 2018 IEEE/WIC/ACM international conference on web intelligence* (pp. 736–739). https://doi.org/10.1109/WI.2018.000-2

Appendix 1

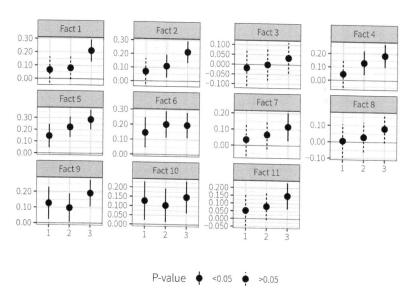

Figure A1 Assessment of fact (robustness check by Coarsened Exact Matching: *cem*).

Note

Baseline is group 0. The abbreviation of fact_x corresponds to the following statements:

Fact 1	ROK used a fire-radar to a patrol plane.	Fact 7	It happened in the Japanese EEZ.
Fact 2	ROK destroyer was searching an NK vessel.	Fact 8	The radar was an action right before firing.
Fact 3	Japan requested ROK to prevent an incident.	Fact 9	Japan was violating international law.
Fact 4	ROK radar was used multiple times.	Fact 10	It was in Korean territorial water.
Fact 5	Japanese plane was flying low.	Fact 11	Japan requested ROK to apologize.
Fact 6	Japanese plane used the radio.		

The bars indicate 95% confidence intervals.

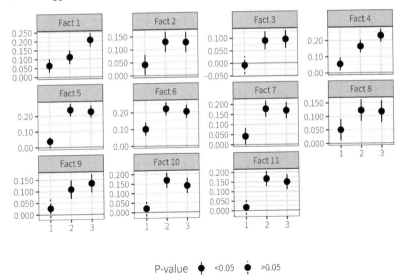

P-value ● <0.05 ● >0.05

Figure A2 Assessment of fact (robustness check by Entropy Balancing: *ebal*).

Note
Baseline is group 0. The abbreviation of fact_x corresponds to the following statements:

Fact 1	ROK used a fire-radar to a patrol plane.	Fact 7	It happened in the Japanese EEZ.
Fact 2	ROK destroyer was searching an NK vessel.	Fact 8	The radar was an action right before firing.
Fact 3	Japan requested ROK to prevent an incident.	Fact 9	Japan was violating international law.
Fact 4	ROK radar was used multiple times.	Fact 10	It was in Korean territorial water.
Fact 5	Japanese plane was flying low.	Fact 11	Japan requested ROK to apologize.
Fact 6	Japanese plane used the radio.		

The bars indicate 95% confidence intervals.

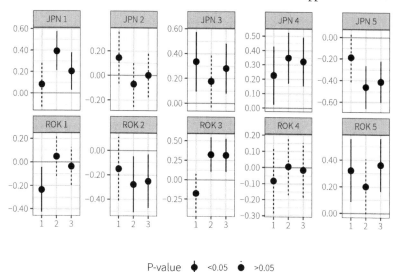

Figure A3 Assessment of two governments (robustness check by Coarsened Exact Matching: *cem*).

Note
Baseline is group 0. The abbreviation of JPN/ROK_x corresponds to the following statements:

JPN/ROK 1	Support the actions by Japanese SDF/Support the actions by the ROK Navy.
JPN/ROK 2	Support the JPN protest against ROK/Support ROK statement to fully explain.
JPN/ROK 3	Feel the political motive of Abe/Feel the political motive of Moon.
JPN/ROK 4	Feel legitimacy about Japanese actions/Feel legitimacy about ROK actions.
JPN/ROK 5	Feel Japanese gov. is hiding something/Feel ROK gov. is hiding something.

The bars indicate 95% confidence intervals.

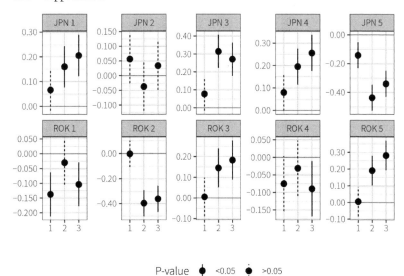

Figure A4 Assessment of two governments (robustness check by Entropy Balancing: *ebal*).

Note
Baseline is group 0. The abbreviation of JPN/ROK_x corresponds to the following statements:

JPN/ROK 1	Support the actions by Japanese SDF/Support the actions by the ROK Navy.
JPN/ROK 2	Support the JPN protest against ROK/Support ROK statement to fully explain.
JPN/ROK 3	Feel the political motive of Abe/Feel the political motive of Moon.
JPN/ROK 4	Feel legitimacy about Japanese actions/Feel legitimacy about ROK actions.
JPN/ROK 5	Feel Japanese gov. is hiding something/Feel ROK gov. is hiding something.

The bars indicate 95% confidence intervals.

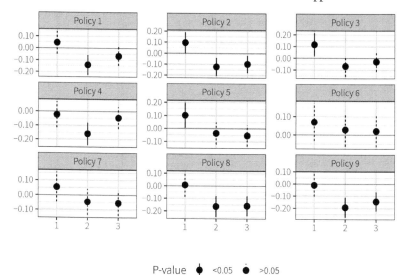

Figure A5 Assessment of potential policies (robustness check by Coarsened Exact Matching: *cem*).

Note
Baseline is group 0. The abbreviation of Policy_x corresponds to the following statements:

Policy 1	Support discreetly solved among the diplomats.	Policy 6	Japan should have reconsidered its countermeasure.
Policy 2	Support discreetly solved among the military.	Policy 7	Japan should have asked the USA to intervene.
Policy 3	Support not solved by top leaders.	Policy 8	Japan should have asked the UN to intervene.
Policy 4	ROK should have apologized.	Policy 9	Japan should have shown clear evidence.
Policy 5	Japan should have reacted in a restricted manner.		

The bars indicate 95% confidence intervals.

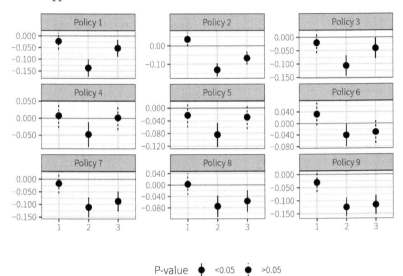

P-value ● <0.05 ● >0.05

Figure A6 Assessment of potential policies (robustness check by Entropy Balancing: *ebal*).

Note
Baseline is group 0. The abbreviation of Policy_x corresponds to the following statements:

Policy 1	Support discreetly solved among the diplomats.	Policy 6	Japan should have reconsidered its countermeasure.
Policy 2	Support discreetly solved among the military.	Policy 7	Japan should have asked the USA to intervene.
Policy 3	Support not solved by top leaders.	Policy 8	Japan should have asked the UN to intervene.
Policy 4	ROK should have apologized.	Policy 9	Japan should have shown clear evidence.
Policy 5	Japan should have reacted in a restricted manner.		

The bars indicate 95% confidence intervals.

Appendix 2

Table A1 Ordinary least squares regressions (Korean sample)

				Issue attitudes		
		Willingness to forgive	ROK should listen to JP	ROK should not make any concessions	The 2015 pact should be kept	The statue in Busan should be removed
				Coef. (B)		
Treatment Baseline: Statement-only	Control	−0.025 (0.015)	0.021 (0.024)	−0.024 (0.018)	0.031 (0.028)	−0.015 (0.020)
	US supports JP	−0.015 (0.015)	−0.025 (0.024)	0.001 (0.018)	−0.061* (0.028)	−0.000 (0.020)
	US supports ROK	−0.003 (0.015)	−0.012 (0.024)	−0.023 (0.018)	0.015 (0.028)	0.010 (0.020)
	US supports JP–ROK pact	−0.013 (0.015)	0.013 (0.024)	−0.005 (0.018)	−0.011 (0.028)	−0.000 (0.020)
Demographic variables	Sex (female)	0.001 (0.010)	−0.013 (0.015)	0.008 (0.012)	−0.101** (0.018)	−0.026* (0.013)
	Age	0.000 (0.000)	0.002* (0.001)	−0.002** (0.001)	−0.000 (0.001)	−0.001+ (0.001)
	Education	−0.025+ (0.013)	0.005 (0.021)	0.036* (0.016)	0.094** (0.025)	0.059** (0.018)
Feeling thermometer	Japan	0.177** (0.030)	−0.243** (0.047)	−0.216** (0.037)	−0.406** (0.056)	−0.265** (0.040)
	Japanese people	0.152** (0.031)	−0.062 (0.049)	0.054 (0.038)	0.153** (0.058)	−0.024 (0.042)
	Constant	0.236** (0.026)	0.638** (0.042)	0.983** (0.032)	0.703** (0.049)	0.920** (0.036)
	Observations	1,300	1,300	1,300	1,300	1,300
	R-squared	0.133	0.063	0.058	0.095	0.082

Standard errors in parentheses

** $p < 0.01$, * $p < 0.05$, + $p < 0.1$

Table A2 Ordinary least squares regressions (Japanese sample)

				Issue attitudes		
		Willingness to forgive	JP should listen to ROK	JP should not make any concessions	The 2015 pact should be kept	The statue in Busan should be removed
				Coef. (B)		
Treatment Baseline: Statement-only	Control	0.033* (0.017)	0.006 (0.022)	0.052* (0.022)	0.001 (0.019)	0.060** (0.022)
	US supports JP	0.023 (0.017)	−0.029 (0.022)	0.038+ (0.022)	0.015 (0.019)	0.048* (0.022)
	US supports ROK	0.018 (0.017)	−0.022 (0.022)	0.030 (0.022)	0.011 (0.019)	0.028 (0.022)
	US supports JP–ROK pact	0.029+ (0.017)	−0.054* (0.022)	0.003 (0.022)	0.050** (0.019)	0.042+ (0.022)
Demographic variables	Sex (female)	−0.008 (0.011)	−0.016 (0.014)	−0.028* (0.014)	0.031* (0.012)	−0.028* (0.014)
	Age	−0.001* (0.001)	0.000 (0.001)	−0.001 (0.001)	0.002** (0.001)	0.003** (0.001)
	Education	−0.028* (0.013)	−0.023 (0.018)	−0.005 (0.018)	0.035* (0.015)	0.037* (0.018)
Feeling thermometer	South Korea	−0.197** (0.039)	−0.274** (0.052)	−0.318** (0.051)	−0.292** (0.044)	−0.370** (0.051)
	South Korean people	−0.134** (0.034)	−0.363** (0.046)	−0.300** (0.045)	0.050 (0.039)	−0.083+ (0.045)
	Constant	0.823** (0.028)	0.777** (0.037)	0.855** (0.036)	0.751** (0.031)	0.730** (0.036)
	Observations	1,298	1,298	1,298	1,298	1,298
	R-squared	0.112	0.206	0.201	0.078	0.135

Standard errors in parentheses

** $p < 0.01$, * $p < 0.05$, + $p < 0.1$

Index

Italicized and **bold** pages refer to figures and tables respectively, and page numbers followed by "n" refer to notes.

For Product Safety Concerns and Information please contact our EU
representative GPSR@taylorandfrancis.com Taylor & Francis Verlag GmbH,
Kaufingerstraße 24, 80331 München, Germany

Printed and bound by CPI Group (UK) Ltd, Croydon, CR0 4YY
11/04/2025
01844011-0007